MW01235105

Credits

Author:
Claudie Marie Holmes

Inspired by:
Almighty God

Graphic Designer:
Derrick Richburg

Publisher:
Independent
ISBN: 979-8-9873837-0-4
ISBN: 979-8-9873837-2-8
ISBN: 979-8-9873837-1-1
ISBN: 979-8-9873837-3-5

Email:
claudieholmes@ymail.com
claudieholmes1210@gmail.com

Table of Contents

Chapter Review

Chapter Review: A short description of each chapter in this book.

My Prayer: I pray that the Lord will speak through me and that the readers will hear from God and be blessed.

Book Cover Explanation: The book cover was given to me in a vision. It is layered with several paradoxes, along with other visual metaphors, double entendre, and subliminal messages. I believe it will speak to every individual in the way that God has intended.

The Reason I Write: I write with the intent to raise awareness of the harmful effects of harsh discipline practices, and to introduce alternative methods of discipline that our Heavenly Father would be proud of.

Introduction: Warning to the readers, this book contains very controversial material that shines a light on the dark and tender topic of child discipline.

My Childhood: My experiences as a child where I was raised in a home of faith. The good, the bad and the ugly.

Emerge: A powerful freedom poem.

I Believe: My beliefs are based upon God's Word. God has placed a deep conviction in my heart and a disputable insight concerning the methods used to teach and discipline His children.

God's Creation: Children are the purest form of man. Children are especially valuable to our God as they are His little disciples and are born for God's purpose.

Don't Cross The Line: It's a thin line between love and hate, punishment and abuse. Parents need to learn to stay in their lane and let God do the rest.

A Better Way: Healthy disciplinary strategies on how to discipline our children.

The Power of The Tongue: Choosing words wisely. The tongue can take life just as quickly as it can give life. The tongue can tear down one's spirit just as easily as it can lift one's spirit up.

Violence Begets Violence: The principle of sowing and reaping: a learned behavior of violence passed from generation to generation. The roots of which extend beyond the era of Moses. Toxic behavior patterns that I believe that have overflowed from slavery, also dating back to B.C. Roman government, extending to our schools, to our homes, to our churches and spills out into society even today.

The Rod of Correction: The (ROC) "Spare The Rod, Spoil The Child", looking at these phases from different perspectives. The heart of this book.

A Wake-up Call: A dream I experienced with God-given interpretation that has compelled me to write this book. Also, an invitation to Christ and the Lord's Prayer.

Believers Believe: Placing total trust in Jesus and standing on the power of God's Word, we are instructed to test the spirit. What is the motivation for our actions?

Testimonial: My previous and current perceptions on the "ROC", my struggles and the benefit of applying these beliefs to my home.

Survey Results: Data and findings, comments and experiences shared from surveys and interviews from others.

Glossary: Defining words used in this book.

favorite Scriptures: Popular Scriptures used in this book and more.

References and Resources
Programs and organizations that can assist those that have been associated with abuse, mental health, parenting strategies and more.

Mental Notes: A place for readers to journal key points that they wish to keep and not forget.

My Prayer

Father God, which is in heaven I come before Your Presence with a heart of thanksgiving, in the humblest way that I know how. My heart, soul and mind are waiting to hear from You. Father God, I am waiting to hear what You would have me share with your people by way of this book.

I pray Father God, that You will give every reader of this book the wisdom and the knowledge to rightly divide the Word of Truth, which is the Word of God, the Holy Bible, in which You, oh God have left for us to live, to move and to have our being by following the principles recorded in it. Your Word is the blueprint for our lives and the compass for our souls, and the map to Your Kingdom.

Father God, I ask that You open the mind of the readers. I pray that You will soften our hearts so that we may hear and receive only those things in which You, Father God, would have us hear.

Lord remove the veils from our eyes so that we may clearly see You. I pray oh Lord, that You will remove any biases and cultural influences. I pray that God will heal any spiritual, emotional, and mental wounds and all psychological scars.

I pray that You will place conviction in our spirits of those things that are not of You so that we can line up with Your perfect will. Father God, I pray that the readers will begin to minister Your Word to their little disciples oh God.

I pray that every reader will be blessed by reading this book and that You Lord God will begin to open doors of blessings in their lives, fulfilling the promises of Your Word and that we will begin to reap the harvest and enjoy the fruit of our labor.

I ask all these things according to Your will, in Your Son Jesus Name Amen.

Book Cover Explanation

The book cover was given to me by God in a vision. It is layered with several paradoxes, along with other visual metaphors, double entendres, and subliminal messages that I believe will speak to every individual in the way that God has intended.

The intentional imperfections of the cross-shaped sword and the heart symbolizes the faults and sins of humankind in which Christ has carried and buried with Him on Calvary.

The sword itself symbolizes the power of love, God's Word, correction, and the sacrifice of Christ Jesus.

The heart symbolizes the spirit and soul of mankind, our consciousness, our desires, and our mindsets.

The green world symbolizes prosperity, healing powers, harmony and peace, immortality, eternal life, new growth, renewal, and resurrection. It is also the color of vegetation and nature.

The New Testament is intentionally positioned in front of the

Old Testament. The New Testament surpasses, outweighs and fulfills the ordinances of the Old Testament. The Old Testament way was condemnation and death. The New Testament is conviction and life. Jesus is the light that brought clarity to reveal the intentions of the Old Testament.

'For the word of God is quick, and powerful, and sharper than any twoedged sword, piercing even to the dividing asunder of soul and spirit, and of the joints and marrow, and is a discerner of the thoughts and intents of the heart.' Hebrews 4:12 KJV

'Foolishness is bound in the heart of a child; But the rod of correction shall drive it far from him.' Proverbs 22:15 KJV

Jesus is the Word of God made flesh. He is The Living Word of God that shows the world and the church the error of our ways. Jesus is the Rock "ROC" of our salvation and the example of how we are to live by love, by faith, by the Spirit, by mercy and by His grace, in the Righteousness of Christ Jesus through the shedding of His Blood.

There is no remission of sin without a sacrifice and the shedding of blood, In both the Old and the New Testament. Jesus is that sacrifice in the New Testament. Romans 12:1 tells us to present our bodies as a living sacrifice to Him today.

'I beseech you therefore, brethren, by the mercies of God, that ye present your bodies a living sacrifice, holy, acceptable unto God, which is your reasonable service. '
Romans 12:1 KJV

The Word of God is for everyone throughout the world whether you are green or purple, old or young, rich or poor. God's Word is a powerful instrument that we are to use to teach, train, correct and discipline our children. It is a spiritual device that is designed to change a person's heart and mind. The Living Word of God is a weapon that enables us to defeat Satan and to save souls from the snares of the Devil and eternal damnation.

The Reason I Write

At the age of 32 God began to reveal to me things that I have felt to be true in my soul all my life. God would wake me up every night speaking to my heart, dropping messages and convictions in my Spirit. He would wake me night after night at the same time urging me to get up. I'm like, "Lord I am trying to sleep", but God was very persistent. I finally surrendered and began to get up, especially since I couldn't sleep anyway, I began to write down the things that He would give me, not realizing at the time it would be used for this very book.

Some of the things that God was sharing with me were not always easy to accept. Even though my heart was feeling like, this is what I was trying to tell you. I still wrestled with it because it went against everything that I was taught my entire life. I realize now that I was more worried about what people would think about me rather than the better way God was showing me.

Deep inside I knew that my parents, family, and church family would not understand nor agree with my convictions. But God confirmed His Word to me through visions and dreams, through the Holy Bible, through speaking with other Believers and non-believer alike, through the events of my life; as well as while I was raising my three children, and even now, helping to raise my grandchildren. Verbal and physical punishment of our children is not the way Jesus intended for parents to discipline His children.

I do not have a Doctorate in Psychology. I am not a Child Counselor, nor do I have any fancy degrees, but I am a child of the Most High God and I have God's Presence in my heart. I know that I cannot of myself help anyone, but the Lord can speak through me to help some. People that know me realize that just writing this book is a miracle. My reading and writing skills are not the best and my speech is not much better. My grades in school were less than average, and I barely graduated high school.

Before starting this book almost 20 years ago, I had probably never read a complete book in my life. When God told me to write this book, "The Rod of Correction". I had to put my total trust in Him because I knew that my abilities alone would not be enough. I knew that my own family would probably doubt me. My friends may think I have lost my mind. My church family may think I have lost "the faith", but I am determined to do what I believe God has called me to do. I will let God be the Judge. So, I am writing this book out of obedience, and through the inspiration of Father God, and the power of the Holy Spirit, in hopes that I can help someone concerning the discipline of our children.

Introduction

This book discusses a very controversial and age-old topic that most people find somewhat difficult to talk about, though the need to talk about it is great. The subject of "child discipline" and whether physical and verbal punishment should or should not be used. This answer can vary from one extreme to another depending on one's belief. An individual's beliefs are influenced by their many experiences and events in life.

This book is intended to understand where some of these beliefs originated from, and whether they are beneficial or not. This book is intended to shine a light on a dark topic and to provide alternate forms of discipline methods.

I have researched and have carried out my own study. I have taken a survey and interviewed hundreds of people concerning the topic of child discipline and its effects on a person. I have shared my findings in this book.

I have also shared my personal beliefs, experiences, and Godly convictions. I aim to reveal how harsh verbal and physical punishment as a form of discipline may seem to work short-term, but may cause long-term damage to a child's spiritual, mental, emotional, physical, and psychological health. Irreparable damage and negative practices that a child experiences may have negative effects throughout their adulthood and be passed on to their children, fostering and continuing a vicious cycle of aggressive behavior.

The Word of God is a Rod and a Sword, as well as a comfort, even in disciplining form. The Great Shepherd. **(See Psalms 23)**. The Bible is the Living Word of God. Jesus Christ is the "ROC" of our salvation. Jesus Christ is the light of the world. The Bible is a spiritual tool that can be understood and used in both the natural and in the spirit realm. The Bible often uses parables and metaphors in comparison to natural things, (things that we can see) which we can compare to spiritual things, (things that we cannot see).

Yes, man has and probably always will use man-made methods and devices to try to control and beat children into submission, just as they did in the days of slavery.

As Believers, we shouldn't discipline our children like the world (society), nor with its weapons. God has commanded me to warn the world, as well as the church of their wrathful ways. I realize everyone will not agree with me, but that's ok, not everyone agreed, believed, or will accept Jesus.

For thousands of years, man has used the Scriptures to justify wrathful behavior. Even many Believers have accepted these teachings to be the truth. God-fearing men and women throughout the world have been blinded by ignorance, doing only what they have been conditioned to do.

This learned behavior has been beaten into us over thousands of years, even before the era of Moses. Many have accepted it as truth, even though deep down in our souls every time we execute this type of punishment, we feel the guilt, the grief, and the shame of it. Yet we turn a blind eye and continue to do so and are teaching others this same vicious cycle. Many people justify their behavior by using the Scriptures out of context. Some make excuses for it by saying things like: God uses harsh discipline. To this I say, we are not God. Some say, "if it was good enough for me then, it's good enough for my children." Others say, "it is showing tough love" or "if I don't, the police will."

Jesus says love is kind, love is patient, love is long suffering, love is merciful, love is forgiving. When we spank our children, although we may mean well, we are not showing these characteristics, but the total opposite.

We are showing our children what behavior is acceptable when someone does something they don't like, or when someone wrongs them. We are turning the child's safe haven into a place of fear and mistrust. The same hand that is supposed to love and protect them is the same hand that is causing them pain, shame, confusion, and anger.

My nephew shared a quote with me after discussing the topic of child discipline, he said: "I would rather have a person that hates me, to treat me as if they love me, than have a person that loves me to treat me as if they hate me".

I don't care what you call it or how you do it, we must see physical and verbal punishment, violence, and abuse for what it is, "wrath". Two wrongs don't make a right. I am convinced that spanking and using the rod of man as a measure of discipline is only a temporary fix and will not bring the desired results over time. I believe that it does more harm than good to our children's physical, spiritual, mental, emotional, and psychological health.

To win against the enemy we must first recognize who the enemy is, and the Lord knows, it is not our children! We need to understand what weapons our enemy uses and what weapons we need to defeat the enemy. These answers and many more can be found in this book and in seeking God's truth for yourself.

My Childhood

I grew up in a Pentecostal, Church of God in Christ (COGIC) home, a home in which; Holiness was the standard with my father, my mother and my four sisters. My Father had a son prior to marrying my mother. Unfortunately, my brother lived outside of our home. The doctors told my mother for years that she would never have children, but after many prayers my parents received their miracle. God blessed them with five live births, five miracles, all girls. I am the fourth born out of the five. Together they had six children. My mom and dad were really hoping that I would have been a junior but as God would have it, I am a beautiful girl. However, I was still named after my dad, I was somewhat a tomboy and a daddy's girl.

My father and my mother were two of the most faithful, God-fearing people that a person could ever meet. My parents were happily married for over 40 years. They loved each other and treated one another with the utmost respect. My four sisters were the smartest, most beautiful, and obedient children a parent could ask for. Me on the other hand, not so much. I have always been very opinionated, inquisitive, and strong-willed. These characteristics were not the best qualities to have as a little girl. My parents loved their family and did everything they knew how to do to provide for us spiritually and financially. We were their little angels.

Dad was a country man with endless talents. I believe there is nothing that my dad could not do. Dad was a trombone-playing Deacon and Trustee of the Church. Dad was a sturdy man, farmer, hunter, fisherman, beekeeper, a hard-working construction worker and a school bus driver with a third-grade education. He was also a salesman and a handyman along with every other job. In today's time, he would have been considered an entrepreneur. He was a gentle giant, with a big heart. He had a huge sense of humor and a calm demeanor.

Mother was the Church Secretary and eventually, she would be appointed a District Missionary of our church. She was a stay-at-home mom and an entrepreneur as well. Mom made and sold arts and crafts. Mom ran a home-daycare for most of my childhood, until she began caring for her mother, my grandmother, who had Alzheimer's Disease. My mother had a sweet and quiet spirit. My mother was a virtuous woman who could make something out of practically nothing.

When handling conflict in their relationship, they made it look so easy. All my life I can tell you that I never heard them even raise their voices at each other. When my mom would express her concerns or frustrations to my dad, he would patiently listen to her, completely hearing her out. That was until she started to nag, then my dad would say in a calm but stern tone, "That is enough, I hear you". My mother would not say another word. Their relationship was one to be desired.

I remember very little of my childhood. I really wish I had more positive memories. What I can tell you is my parents loved us, and only wanted the best for us and that included our soul salvation. They loved the Lord and loved going to church. Long as we lived under their roof, when they went to church, we went to church. Whether we wanted to or not. leaving little room for us to get into devilment or idol time.

Back then, in the 60's & 70's it was not unusual to attend church every day of the week and twice on Sundays. This left very little time for homework and chores; so, watching TV, playing around, dating, and getting into mischief was almost non-existent. Church and school is where we spent the majority of our time; therefore, church and school is where I got into the most trouble.

My parents were very strict, which is an understatement. Remember, my parents grew up in the era and areas of segregation, oppression, recession, and the effects of slavery were not far removed. They faithfully believed: "Spare The Rod and Spoil The Child". If the Bible said it, that settled it. If the preachers said it, then it was fact, no questions asked, especially considering their educational background. They just wholeheartedly wanted to please the Lord. My parents were faithful to the church and even more faithful to God. The standards in our home were set so high that I have always felt like they were impossible to achieve. The pressure of living up to these expectations almost drove me insane. We had more rules than the pastor's own children.

The rules that they set were supposedly Scripturally based. Being girls, we were only allowed to wear dresses, no shorts, or pants, for the longest time, even during P.E. This belief was based on their perspective and teaching of the following verse:

'A woman shall not wear anything that pertains to a man, nor shall a man put on a woman's garment, for all who do so are an abomination to the Lord your God.' Deuteronomy 22:5 NKJV

We could not go to any out-of-school time events such as: Games, dances, or proms. We could barely go to a family member's house; therefore, going to a friend's house was out of the question. We didn't dare ask to go to the mall or the movies, which would have *been a waste of breath. It was considered a sin, because supposedly, we would have been sitting in the seat of the scornful.*

*When it came to a*sking about going anywhere other than church, it didn't matter what we asked them, they never gave an immediate answer. Mom would tell us to ask dad, and dad in return would ask us, "What did your mom say"? Both of them would always have to pray about it first. That is just how unified they were and how serious they were about hearing from God.

Blessed is the man Who walks not in the counsel of the ungodly, Nor stands in the path of sinners, Nor sits in the seat of the scornful; Psalms 1:1 NKJV

As I entered my teenage years, I got to know God for myself and read God's Word for myself. When I read the Bible, it was like the words would just lift off the pages and dance before me. God would make the Scriptures so simple, and as clear as a picture on a wall. It was the book that I could actually read and understand. I would get so excited. I began to share with my parents the things that I believed God had shown me concerning the Scriptures.

My experience was that it happened, that some of the things God had shown me were about the Scriptures that my parents were using to enforce their rules, and how they were being used out of context. They took it as if I was challenging their authority. I'm sure you can imagine, that did not workout so well for me. Before long I lost the desire to read the Bible and share His Word. I quickly learned to silence my voice. It has taken a lifetime and the power of the Holy Spirit to find it again.

We would get whipped for misbehaving, lying, stealing, speaking out of turn, getting bad grades in school and for me, fighting was a big one. I fought so much and so well that the school kids gave me a nickname, "SugarRay-Claudie".

I was the only one out of my sisters that would get whippings for fighting and bad grades, my sisters were very smart, but no matter how hard I tried to get good grades, I still got bad grades.

I was the only left-handed person in my family as well, which put me at a total disadvantage. My sisters would try to help me read and write better but it wasn't of much help. Also, it didn't help matters that the majority of the time I was doing my homework from a church pew.

Report card day was terrifying. So, I started changing my F's to A's on my report card to stop the spanking but that only lasted for so long before they would catch on. Later in life I would learn that I have a learning disability and all those whippings were for something that was out of my control.

Physical discipline in our home was a big ordeal. It didn't happen that often but when it did, it was a memorable experience; what I can truthfully say is that, for the most part, we didn't get whipped at the time of the offense. I always figured it was their time to cool down and pray or something. They would re-address the situation at a later time. It was always sometime before they went to bed.

"Be angry, and do not sin": do not let the sun go down on your wrath,
Ephesians 4:26 NKJV

There have been occasions where we thought they had forgotten all about it; but nope, they never did. They would call us into their office, which was their bedroom; they would explain why they were whipping us. They would tell us that they loved us, which by the way was the only time that they would verbally express their love. Then they would tell us: "This is going to hurt us more than it hurts you". After that speech, we had to get into position, which most of the time was bedside on our knees and my dad would proceed to whip us with a belt, or a branch off of a tree while my mother watched.

My sisters would cry and wail. I would never shed a tear or mumble a sound, no matter how bad it hurt. It just made me so furious inside. I couldn't understand it; it felt nothing like love. It was not in their character to do such a thing as showing affectionate love. In my mind, there was nothing that we had done so badly that we deserved that type of punishment. It was not that we didn't deserve to be disciplined, but I felt that this was crossing the line.

Sometimes we would get up with bruises and welts. I thought about calling the abuse hotline on a few occasions, sometimes even with the phone in my hand. I think the only thing that stopped me was the fear of God, the fear of being split up from my sisters or getting into an even worse situation; because when it is all said and done, I believe that our parents loved us, and they were doing what the "Bible" told them to do. This made absolutely no sense to me and put a bad taste in my mouth for God.

I have spent the majority of my childhood angry and confused, trying to fit in a box that was too small for me. I suffered from severe self-esteem issues and exhibited an "I don't care attitude". As a result, I went searching for love and made some bad choices because of these confusing experiences.

I know my parents loved us and they just wanted to protect us and to keep us saved from sin. I truly believe that my parents' teaching us the love and fear of God was more beneficial than any whipping that they could have ever given. I appreciate everything my parents did for us; however, I also truly believe that if they knew a better way to discipline us, they would have done so.

There is one whipping that I will never forget. I do not remember what my sister and I did, but whatever it was, it must have been very bad because we received the beating of our lives. I remember my dad making us get into a very large, sweet potato sack, half-naked and we were beaten with a fishing rod.

My sister cried and wailed, as usual. However, I still didn't shed a tear. It was not until I heard my sister crying in the bathroom and I saw the bleeding lacerations on her back that I cried.

My parents were not monsters, DO NOT read this story out of context; like many other people do all the time with the Scriptures. They used the Bible out of their own misunderstanding while believing that they were doing the right thing.

Reading this story without considering the era of time, without understanding why, or without knowing their true character, could easily seem that they were mean, but they were not that way. Remember, I have described their characteristics at the beginning of this story.

My parents were wonderful, God-fearing, loving people. No, they were not perfect, but they certainly were striving to the best of their understanding to be the best and I wouldn't have traded them for the world.

They were only doing what they knew to do and what they believed was the right thing to do, while being blinded and influenced by religious and environmental biases.

Many times, Scriptures were used out of context because of the lack of education and knowledge on the part of their religious trail blazers. My parents were and are not the only parents that meant well and desired only the best life for their children but are going about it all wrong.

Jesus says, this is not His will or His way. God is love, merciful, longsuffering, forgiving, and kind.

After I completed a few chapters of my book. I wanted to give it to my mother to read but I was so afraid, afraid of rejection. I didn't want to disappoint her with my non-traditional beliefs. But the urge was so strong that in spite of my fears, I gave it to my mom to read. My dad had already transitioned by that time. I didn't know if my mom would read it or not, but to my surprise she did.

After a few days she came to me and apologized for how they disciplined us. I cannot put into words how that made me feel. Even as an adult, that moment was priceless. I felt valued and heard for the very first time and it was all because I had shared the things that

God had shared with me. I never would have in a million years believed that my mother would have responded to my book in such a way, I know it could have only been God.

When it comes to discipline, God has taken my most painful memories from my childhood and used them to catapult me into my God-given purpose. God has given me the soul conviction along with the heart desire to help others to bring about a change. I am motivated by my own childhood pain but driven by the pain of others.

Emerge

Poem: By Claudie Holmes (11/01/2019)

Significant although diminutive.
Submerged with a purpose.
Under pressure with a plan.
Alone and confused.
Which way is up?
Which way is down?
Suffocating with darkness all
around.
Scared to live yet afraid to die.
My instincts Emerge.

Predestined to live I fight.
Out of this desolate place, full of
despair, I Emerge.
From the dust and dirt where
once I was imprisoned, leaving it
all beneath me.
Where darkness once ruled.
I am donned with the glorious
and radiant light from the
heavens.
Where I was once engulfed with
fear.
I have the freedom to love, to
grow, and to thrive.

Days have come, years have
passed.
The heavens seem to be just in
my grasp.
I have given myself without
reservation; shade and shelter,
food and medicine, pleasure, and
protection.

I am great.
I am grand.
I soar in the sky.
I sway with the wind.
I am strong.
Nothing can move me.
Nothing shall shake me.

For as much as I emerge, I am
submerged.
For I am free, but not free.
For I am anchored by the Source,
the Sustainer of true life.
To truly live, is to truly love.
To become truly free, is to truly
die.
For I shall finally, for all
eternity…… Emerge.

I Believe

I Believe:
As believers, what we believe may not matter to others. What we believe matters to God! In fact, our faith means everything to Him.

But without faith it is impossible to please Him, for he who comes to God must believe that He is, and that He is a rewarder of those who diligently seek Him. Hebrews 11:6 NKJV

I Believe:
The **R**od **O**f **C**orrection, "ROC", which is used in Proverbs 22:15 is a metaphor God uses as an illustration of the power of using the Holy Bible as a correcting tool.

'Foolishness is bound in the heart of a child; But the rod of correction shall drive it far from him.' Proverbs 22:15 NKJV

I Believe:
That the word "rod" which is used in Proverbs 22:15 is used in a similar manner, in which the Word of God

describes the sword of the Spirit in Ephesians 6:17.

'And take the helmet of salvation, and the sword of the Spirit, which is the word of God:'
Ephesians 6:17 KJV

I Believe:
The Bible is a spiritual tool that we should use to discipline our children.

'All scripture is given by inspiration of God, and is profitable for doctrine, for reproof, for correction, for instruction in righteousness: '
2 Timothy 3:16 KJV

I Believe:
Believers should not discipline God's little disciples like the world, nor with its weapons. Children are not our enemy.

'For we wrestle not against flesh and blood, but against principalities, against powers, against the rulers of the darkness of this world, against spiritual wickedness in high places. '
Ephesians 6:12 KJV

I Believe:
The **R**od **O**f **C**orrection "ROC" in Proverbs 23:13-14 is a descriptive

phrase that God uses to state how powerful the Word of God is, as illustrated in Hebrew 4:12.

'Withhold not correction from the child: For if thou beatest him with the rod, he shall not die. Thou shalt beat him with the rod, And shalt deliver his soul from hell. '
Proverbs 23:13-14 KJV

'For the word of God is quick, and powerful, and sharper than any two-edged sword, piercing even to the dividing asunder of soul and spirit, and of the joints and marrow, and is a discerner of the thoughts and intents of the heart. ' Hebrews 4:12 KJV

I Believe:

The "rod" used in Proverbs 23:13-14 describes spiritual weapons and not the earthly weapons used by the culture such as: Sticks and branches, belts, whips, shoes, hands, extension cords or other such things as we have been conditioned to think.

'Now we have received, not the spirit of the world, but the spirit which is of God; that we might know the things that are freely given to us of God. Which things also we speak, not in

the words which man's wisdom teacheth, but which the Holy Ghost teacheth; comparing spiritual things with spiritual.'
1 Corinthians 2:12-13 KJV

I Believe:

That if we love our children, we must correct our children and not leave them to their own wisdom, but to teach them and instruct them by using God's manual for our lives, which is Jesus, the "ROC", the Living Word of God from a young age.

'He who spares his rod hates his son, But he who loves him disciplines him promptly.'
Proverbs 13:24 NKJV

'For their Redeemer is mighty; He will plead their cause against you. Apply your heart to instruction, and your ears to words of knowledge. Do not withhold correction from a child, For if you beat him with a rod, he will not die." Proverbs 23:11-13 NKJV

I Believe:

Satan twists the truth to make it a lie. He uses the Word of God for his own agenda. Just like he did from the very beginning with Adam and Eve and with

Jesus. He mixes a little bit of truth with a whole lot of lies.

And the serpent said unto the woman, Ye shall not surely die: for God doth know that in the day ye eat thereof, then your eyes shall be opened, and ye shall be as gods, knowing good and evil. Genesis 3:4-5 KJV

I Believe:

The words: whipping and spanking are names used instead of physical violence, anger, and wrath. When we whip our children, we are instilling anger and aggression in their hearts.

'And, ye fathers, provoke not your children to wrath: but bring them up in the nurture and admonition of the Lord.' Ephesians 6:4 KJV

I Believe:

Wrath belongs to God.
God has not made man responsible for physically hurting or harming our children or anyone else in any way to make them obey.

'Beloved, do not avenge yourselves, but rather give place to wrath; for it is written,

"Vengeance is Mine, I will repay," says the Lord. '
Romans 12:19 NKJV

'For God hath not appointed us to wrath, but to obtain salvation by our Lord Jesus Christ, '
1 Thessalonians 5:9 KJV

I Believe:

Physical and verbal punishment should not be used as a last result when other methods have failed. Frustrations may be higher at this point; therefore, is even more of a reason to be avoided.

'A man of great wrath shall suffer punishment: For if thou deliver him, yet thou must do it again.' Proverbs 19:19 KJV

I Believe:

God's plan for parents is that parents are to be teachers, instructors, and to correct a child not physical punishment.

'Therefore shall ye lay up these my words in your heart and in your soul, and bind them for a sign upon your hand, that they may be as frontlets between your eyes. And ye shall teach them to your children, speaking of them when thou sittest in thine house, and when thou walkest by the way, when thou liest down, and

when thou risest up. And thou shalt write them upon the door posts of thine house, and upon thy gates: ' Deuteronomy 11:18-20 KJV

I Believe:

Parents and grandparents are called to instill the reverential fear of God in our children, not the fear of parents or of a whipping, or severe punishment. There is nothing or no one that we should teach our children to fear, except the reverential fear of God. If the reverential respect for God is in a child's heart, it will keep their souls forever. They will know that God's eyes are in every place, even when their parent's eyes are not.

'The eyes of the LORD are in every place, Beholding the evil and the good. ' Proverbs 15:3 KJV

'And fear not them which kill the body but are not able to kill the soul: but rather fear him which is able to destroy both soul and body in hell.' Matthew 10:28 KJV

I Believe:

When we spank our children, we are not acting in the spirit but in the flesh (emotions). It can cause bottled up aggression, and a child's spirit may become broken.

'for the wrath of man worketh not the righteousness of God.' James 1:20 KJV

'Fathers, provoke not your children to anger, lest they be discouraged.' Colossians 3:21 KJV

I Believe:
The spanking of our children seems to help for a short time, but only does more harm than good in the long run.

'He who sows iniquity will reap sorrow, And the rod of his anger will fail.' Proverbs 22:8 NKJV

I Believe:
That mutual respect can be lost when parents whip their children. It is hard to love, respect and obey someone that assaults you and whom you feel has disrespected you.

*'A wrathful man stirreth up strife: But he that is slow to anger appeaseth strife. '
Proverbs 15:18 KJV*

I Believe:

A loving parent should model good behavior. They should use positive reinforcements and incentives, positive correction and discipline.

'Let no man despise thy youth; but be thou an example of the believers, in word, in conversation, in charity, in spirit, in faith, in purity.' 1 Timothy 4:12 KJV

'The heart of the wise teacheth his mouth, And addeth learning to his lips. Pleasant words are as a honeycomb, Sweet to the soul, and health to the bones.' Proverbs 16:23-24 KJV

I Believe:

We should treat our children the way we would like to be treated and the way they should treat others.

'Therefore, whatever you want men to do to you, do also to them, for this is the Law and the Prophets.' Matthew 7:12 NKJV

I Believe:

Parents are responsible for leading their children to the living water, but as the parent, I'm not responsible for making them drink. God gives our children the same love, patience, mercy, and free will that He gives us. It is to hear and obey His Word and be rewarded; or to hear and be disobedient and deal with the consequences.

'For the wages of sin is death; but the gift of God is eternal life through Jesus Christ our Lord.' Romans 6:23 KJV

I Believe:

A parent's job is to instill in their children the fear of the Lord and the love of God, which only comes from teaching them God's word.

'Gather the people together, men, and women, and children, and thy stranger that is within thy gates, that they may hear, and that they may learn, and fear the LORD your God, and observe to do all the words of this law: and that their children, which have not known anything, may hear, and learn to fear the LORD your God, as long as ye live in the land whither ye go over Jordan to possess it.'
Deuteronomy 31:12-13 KJV

I Believe:

The way God wants us to beat our children with the "rod" is with the Holy Bible, the Living Word, Jesus is the "ROC". Proverbs 23:12-14 is not a physical beating, but a spiritual beating with His Word. Eternal life only is available through salvation by believing in Christ Jesus' finished work at Calvary. He is the only One Who can free a person's soul from hell, not a whipping.

'Apply thine heart unto instruction, And thine ears to the words of knowledge. Withhold not correction from the child: For if thou beatest him with the rod, he shall not die. Thou shalt beat him with the rod, And shalt deliver his soul from hell." Proverbs 23:12-14 KJV

I Believe:

The words beating, beat it, and beat used in Proverbs 23:12-14 is not talking about a physical beating. A physical beating can absolutely kill a child. However, it is used in a manner in which God wants us to use His Word as an instrument of correction, by constantly over and over, diligently speaking and teaching the Word of God.

'and thou shalt teach them diligently unto thy children, and shalt talk of them when thou sittest in thine house, and when thou walkest by the way, and when thou liest down, and when thou risest up. And thou shalt bind them for a sign upon thine hand, and they shall be as frontlets between thine eyes. And thou shalt write them upon the posts of thy house, and on thy gates. ' Deuteronomy 6:7-9 KJV

I Believe:

God wants His Believers to beat their children by repeatedly speaking God's Word, day and night. Talking to them, singing the Word to them, reading the Word to them, writing the Word with them, hanging them on the walls, until His Word takes root in our children's heart, mind and soul.

'Only take heed to thyself, and keep thy soul diligently, lest thou forget the things which thine eyes have seen, and lest they depart from thy heart all the days of thy life: but teach them thy sons, and thy sons' sons; specially the day that thou stoodest before the LORD thy God in Horeb, when the LORD said unto me, Gather me the people together, and I will make them hear my words, that they may learn to fear me

*all the days that they shall live upon the earth,
and that they may teach their children.'
Deuteronomy 4:9-10 KJV*

I Believe:

The whipping of our children today can
be traced back to before the time of
Moses, when physical beating was used
to keep discipline, and for correction,
and to control people with fear and
torment. This method of discipline has
been passed down from generation to
generation and must be stopped. Just
because our parents did it, didn't make it
right then, and does not make it right
now.

*'Cease from anger, and forsake wrath; Do not
fret— it only causes harm.' Psalms 37:8 NKJV*

I Believe:

When we speak words, we release the
most powerful weapon we have against
disobedience in our lives and our
children's lives - Proverbs 18:21.

*'Death and life are in the power of the tongue:
And they that love it shall eat the fruit thereof. '
Proverbs 18:21 KJV*

'Your word is a lamp to my feet And a light to my path.' Psalms 119:105 NKJV

I Believe:

Biblical affirmations are powerful tools that can help shape the hearts and minds of our children as well as our own. Repeatedly speaking those things that God has spoken over our lives instills a spiritual belief which influences behavior.

'My son, give attention to my words; Incline your ear to my sayings. Do not let them depart from your eyes; Keep them in the midst of your heart; For they are life to those who find them, And health to all their flesh.'
Proverbs 4:20-22 NKJV

I Believe:

Whipping our children demonstrates the opposite of everything Jesus has called us to be. We should display the fruit of the spirit.

'But the fruit of the Spirit is love, joy, peace, longsuffering, gentleness, goodness, faith, meekness, temperance: against such there is no law. ' Galatians 5:22-23 KJV

I Believe:

When we yell and scream, curse and make idle threats, and use other harsh tones and words to discipline our children, we are not pleasing God.

'A soft answer turneth away wrath: But grievous words stir up anger. The tongue of the wise useth knowledge aright: But the mouth of fools poureth out foolishness. '
Proverbs 15:1-2 KJV

'Let no corrupt communication proceed out of your mouth, but that which is good to the use of edifying, that it may minister grace unto the hearers. ' Ephesians 4:29 KJV

I Believe:

Children are God's little disciples and a precious gift from God to us and are here for His purpose.

'Whoever receives one little child like this in My name receives Me. "Whoever causes one of these little ones who believe in Me to sin, it would be better for him if a millstone were hung around his neck, and he were drowned in the depth of the sea. '
Matthew 18:5-6 NKJV

Saying, "Do not touch My anointed ones, And do My prophets no harm."
I Chronicles 16:22 NKJV

I Believe:

Parents are their children's covering until they are old enough to understand and seek God for themselves. Parents are God's first defense against the evils of this world.

'Thorns and snares are in the way of the perverse; He who guards his soul will be far from them. Train up a child in the way he should go, And when he is old he will not depart from it.' Proverbs 22:5-6 NKJV

I Believe:

Even if you believe that God meant at one time that we should literally beat our children, you should also believe that God had a change of heart through Jesus Christ. God doesn't change but his methods do. God sent us a better way, through Christ Jesus.

'For Christ is the end of the law for righteousness to every one that believeth.' Romans 10:4 KJV

'Let all bitterness, and wrath, and anger, and clamour, and evil speaking, be put away from you, with all malice: and be ye kind one to another, tenderhearted, forgiving one another, even as God for Christ's sake hath forgiven you.' Ephesians 4:31-32 KJV

I Believe:

We should consult God on how to discipline our children and really wait to hear His answer. Keep an open heart because it will probably require a lot of love, patience, faith and trust on the parent's or guardian's part.

'Trust in the Lord with all your heart, And lean not on your own understanding; In all your ways acknowledge Him, And He shall direct your paths.' Proverbs 3:5-6 NKJV

God's Creation

Do you know how special your child is, and that each child that comes into this world is unique? There's no one in the world just like your child, even identical twins are unique in many ways. God has created your child for His purpose and not your own.

Children are God's creation. Looking upon the face of your child is like looking upon the face of God.

'So God created man in His own image; in the image of God He created him; male and female He created them.' Genesis 1:27 NKJV

We are so precious to God that He did not just speak us into existence like He did everything else. God made it personal. He took the time to handcraft us. God placed a portion of Himself into each and every one of us. Children are created in the likeness of the Heavenly Father.

'And the Lord God formed man of the dust of the ground, and breathed into his nostrils the breath of life; and man became a living being.'
Genesis 2:7 NKJV

Children are the purest form of man. Children are a precious gift from God. As with any gift we should show our appreciation for it. However, children are not just any gift, but a gift from God Himself. God not only expects our appreciation but commands it. The Bible is full of instructions and guidelines on how to do just that, and he intends for us to follow them.

'Behold, children are a heritage from the Lord, The fruit of the womb is a reward.'
Psalms 127:3 NKJV

God has placed parents in a special place in the lives of His little ones. Children are his little disciples. They are the humble, the small, the poor, the frail, the weak and the least, which in God's eyes makes children the greatest. God has placed parents in a position of authority and leadership over our children.

Unfortunately, as with any person in a position of power, there can be good leadership and there can be bad leadership.

Just because we oversee someone doesn't give us the right to abuse that authority. Some parents get the superiority complex, treating our children like they are inferior. In some ways parents may be in a superior role. As parents we may have the wisdom and knowledge that our children may not have, but children are no less valuable.

A good parent will always recognize the potential of their child and impart values, fine tuning and making a deposit into the child's development. Remember, a child/student is only as good as their teacher.

'At that time the disciples came to Jesus, saying, "Who then is greatest in the kingdom of heaven?" Then Jesus called a little child to Him, set him in the midst of them, and said, "Assuredly, I say to you, unless you are converted and become as little children, you will by no means enter the kingdom of heaven. Therefore whoever humbles himself as this

little child is the greatest in the kingdom of heaven. '
Matthew 18:1-4 NKJV, Mark 10:15 NKJV

Although children may be small in size, they are still humans, and God has given our children human feelings and emotions just as he has given to us. Most children just want to be loved, accepted, and appreciated. As parents, we should learn to be empathetic, putting ourselves in their shoes, even when it comes to discipline.

As an adult, how would you feel if someone you loved hit you all in the name of love? Why would our children feel any different about that kind of physical contact, regardless of the reason?

If you hit any adult in the same manner that we hit our children we would most likely be in jail, charged with a crime, or even hit back. But yet we spank, hit and beat the people that are the most vulnerable and the least able to defend themselves. As a matter of fact, we hit our children and expect them to ignore their natural instinct of self-preservation of defending themselves. We expect them to just take it, not to cry or cause a scene, not to feel angry about it, and to love and thank us for it.

Food For Thought:
If you wanted to train a dog to be aggressive, how would you do that? I would be aggressive to the dog. Hitting and yelling at a dog stimulates its fight or flight instincts. Over time I will produce an aggressive dog or a very timid dog. A timid dog can be just as dangerous as an aggressive dog, because a timid dog trust no one and is afraid of everything. It will strike out of fear without warning. Whereas, most aggressive dogs are mean, sending out signals like growling, barking and body language that lets you know to beware.

To train a dog to be loving and obedient you would be loving and kind, you would use incentives and positive correction and reinforcements. I have said all of that to say this; our children are not much different. How we train a child matters. Aggressive punishment will most likely produce an aggressive child. Love, praise, and proper correction produces a loving and obedient child many times over the course of time.

We wonder why our children run to the world. The community can sometimes be more forgiving and accepting than the church. Maybe our children feel that people outside of their home show them more support and respect. Perhaps society is not beating them or being judgmental. Maybe the street is the one place where they can release all the bottled-up anger and aggressive behavior that they have learned from the harsh discipline that they have received at home. Sometimes they may feel more love from outside influences and strangers than they do from their family. Godly love draws people in. Harshness and hostile behavior drives them away.

As God-lead parents, we are to be good stewards over our children and bring them up in adoration and the admonition of the Lord.

This can pose a challenge to many parents because it is easier said than done. Every child is different and unique. God has gifted every child with different personalities, temperaments, with different talents and gifts. Each child enters our lives with their own set of strengths and weaknesses. Children can have characteristics or traits quite different from their parents. Therefore, it is crucial that parents strive to recognize, understand, and cultivate each child's individual needs. A parent must learn to speak their child's love language.

If you're thinking that's tough, that's not even half the battle as most parents are still trying to figure themselves out. We are still working through our own issues, strengths, weaknesses, and faith. These challenges can be very frustrating at times. However, it helps to remember that our children are God's craftsmanship and so are we. God knows exactly what each child needs. We must constantly lean on God for wisdom in order to be the parents that God needs us to be. We must look to the Holy Spirit for guidance and His understanding and not our own.

'For we are His workmanship, created in Christ Jesus for good works, which God prepared beforehand that we should walk in them.'
Ephesians 2:10 NKJV

'Children, obey your parents in the Lord: for this is right. Honor thy father and mother; which is the first commandment with promise; that it may be well with thee, and thou mayest live long on the earth. And, ye fathers, provoke not your children to wrath: but bring them up in the nurture and admonition of the Lord. '
Ephesians 6:1-4 KJV

Don't Cross The Line

As parents and guardians when it comes to figuring out what is right for your family, the lines sometimes seem to become gray and maybe even a little blurry. It is essential that the lines, however faint they are, that we **DO NOT** cross them.

As parents, grandparents, and guardians our job may not be an easy one, but it is one of the most important jobs on the planet. Parents should provide the love and support needed to develop the critical attributes a child needs to live and thrive in this sometimes-cruel world, and for all throughout eternity.

A parent's duties are serious business under God's law, as well as man's law. If a parent fails to meet these responsibilities or overstep their boundaries, the consequences can be catastrophic, followed by long-lasting negative effects that can be devastating to the entire family and society as a whole.

Before even thinking about becoming a parent, one should weigh the pros and the cons. Are you really ready? Research the rights and responsibilities expected of a parent under the laws of their state. The Bible is a great source in understanding the specific role that the parents play in a faith-filled home, and what God says He will do when parents and children follow His instructions, and the consequences if they don't.

A parent is responsible for the love and protection of their children's physical, spiritual, emotional, and mental well-being. A parent is responsible for providing the basic needs, and financial support. They should provide food, shelter and clothing, a bed, medicine, etc. They should ensure a safe environment for their children.

A parent should avoid exposing their children to potential hurt and pain. Parents should warn their children of what can happen in a given situation, by telling them how to avoid certain incidents. The parents should, as much as lies within their power, provide safety for the children by removing and correcting potential known areas of danger and threats.

Parents should teach their children moral values that will help them to develop positive characteristics such as: respect for others as well as themselves, honesty, patience, compassion, forgiveness, responsibility, loyalty, generosity, and integrity, etc.

They should teach their children basic survival skills, proper hygiene practices, as well as good communication skills and share in teaching and providing support in meeting their educational needs. Parents should provide age-appropriate, effective discipline that is fair, structured, and consistent.

Discipline can be the fine line that many parents struggle with. The balance between tough love and abuse sometimes seem to blend together in the moment of desperation and despair. Often times a parent may fall back into the pattern of harshness. In a parents' efforts to make children behave in a way that we want them to or even need them to, followed by the guilt and shame of losing control in the moment.

We know children will misbehave, they are still learning, but so are we. Parents must figure out what to do about our children's misconduct without hurting or harming our children physically, spiritually, mentally, or emotionally. If we don't, The Department of Children and Family (DCF) may soon be knocking at our doors.

Can you recall that old saying, "Sticks and stones may break my bones, but words will never hurt me"? If that isn't a lie, then I don't know what is. Words absolutely do hurt. What we say matters and how we say it. Yelling and screaming, calling names, and swearing at children can cause emotional pain or shame, and can affect a child's self-esteem. This type of discipline dances along the lines of verbal abuse. This too is a line you **DO NOT** want to cross.

Food For Thought:

What do you believe is the determining factor between verbal abuse and physical punishment? When can it be defined as wrath instead of discipline? Is it how mad you are? Is it how loud you yell? Is it which curse word you use? Is it how hard you hit them, and how long or how fast? Is it determined by which device you use, or maybe if physical marks are left on the child? But what about the marks and scars you can't see?

Spanking and physical punishment of any kind increases the risk of injury, scratches, bruises, and broken bones. Spanking can cause lasting-measurable marks physically on a child as well as mentally, emotionally, and spiritually. Flirting into this line of behavior can be detrimental. **DO NOT CROSS THIS LINE!**

As parents we are legally responsible for our children's safety and well-being and even our child's behavior; this may vary from state to state. In cases of abuse, neglect, and abandonment, parents run the risk of having their parental rights terminated under the law. Their children may be removed from their care and there is also a huge possibility of the parents facing criminal charges and being sentenced to prison. God is not pleased with this type of discipline; He gets no Glory from this.

Using aggressive discipline only produces a negative outcome for everyone.

If we are honest with ourselves, we really are not always aware of our own strength when emotions are running rampant, especially when it comes to physical contact with someone much smaller in size than we are.

I do not believe that harsh discipline practices are the will of God. God has given free will to us all, that includes our children. He has set before us rewards and consequences. However, those who will not take correction and warning, they may be met with a "rod" of some kind as a result of their own decisions.

Parents should stay in their lane, after fulfilling their responsibilities in the child's life, while trusting the Lord to produce what only He can produce in the final outcome. Parents should let the Holy Spirit lead and guide them on how they should discipline their children before they too are met with the same "rod".

'And He spoke a parable to them: "Can the blind lead the blind? Will they not both fall into the ditch? ' Luke 6:39 NKJV

'A disciple is not above his teacher, but everyone who is perfectly trained will be like his teacher. And why do you look at the speck in your brother's eye, but do not perceive the plank in your own eye? Or how can you say to your brother, 'Brother, let me remove the speck that is in your eye,' when you yourself do not see the plank that is in your own eye? Hypocrite! First remove the plank from your own eye, and then you will see clearly to remove the speck that is in your brother's eye.' Luke 6:40-42 NKJV

Parents should be careful that the good and bad, right and wrong lines are not blurred. In some instances, lines crossed could yield severe consequences for ourselves, our children, and their children, negatively affecting society at large.

We are in spiritual warfare, but our children are not our enemies. Even if at times it seems as if we are battling with them as with enemies, Jesus even teaches us to love our enemies, and to be kind to them, to do good to them, to pray for them, to turn the other cheek. We must fight this fight with spiritual weapons and not the weapons of man.

There is no place in Christ's earthly life where he condones physical assault on any one person, but especially not on children. He didn't even condone retaliation for the soldiers that crucified Him. Jesus rebuked with words and in modeling unexpected behavior.

Parents must stay in their lane and not play God's role. Leave the wrath in God's hands. God has shown me "A Better Way." A way that does not grieve the Holy Spirit and does not risk spiritual pollutants and physical harm. A way that will free us from the guilt and shame of having to yell and whip our children, and I pray that He will do the same for you. The Holy Spirit is an excellent teacher.

'Finally, my brethren, be strong in the Lord, and in the power of his might. Put on the whole armour of God, that ye may be able to stand against the wiles of the devil. For we wrestle not against flesh and blood, but against principalities, against powers, against the rulers of the darkness of this world, against spiritual wickedness in high places . Wherefore take unto you the whole armour of God, that ye may be able to withstand in the evil day, and having done all, to stand. Stand therefore, having your loins girt about with truth, and having on the breastplate of righteousness; and your feet shod with the preparation of the gospel of peace; above all, taking the shield of faith, wherewith ye shall be able to quench all the fiery darts of the wicked. And take the helmet of salvation, and the sword of the Spirit, which is the word of God: praying always with all prayer and supplication in the Spirit, and watching thereunto with all perseverance and supplication for all saints; '
Ephesians 6:10-18 KJV

If you feel that another adult is abusing your child or his or her own

child, you can call the Child help USA National Child Abuse Hot Line at (800) 422-4453, for advice. If you're certain of the problem, contact your local Child Protective Services (CPS) agency to report it. CPS professionals will evaluate the report, and if they deem it necessary, they will send someone out to talk with the alleged abuser. CPS will keep your report confidential, although you can make an anonymous report if you prefer. But keep in mind that false anonymous reports are, unfortunately, quite common.

Many other helpful resources are available (see References and Resources chapter).

A Better Way

The topic of child discipline can be a very sensitive topic, and depending on your upbringing, it can literally be a painful one. It is an age-old subject, that for generations has caused much controversy over the years and the consequences have been irreparable.

Child discipline is primarily governed by a parent's own conscience. It is an event that usually takes place behind closed doors. It is a topic that is often just swept under the proverbial rug, but somehow remains the elephant in the room in which children are the focus group of concern.

I believe that generally, most parents love their children and want to do the best job they can at training and teaching them.

I believe that subconsciously, many parents intend to produce the best reflection of themselves through their children.

I believe that most parents try to give them the best things in life. We tell ourselves that we are going to be better parents, even if we believe our parents were the best.

When it comes to discipline, we tend to revert back to what we have been taught through our past experiences, when in fact, we truly wanted to do better by our children.

One of the biggest duties we have as parents is teaching our children right from wrong, good from bad. This is no easy task. It requires a lot of love, even more patience, and tons of self-control.

There are many resources that are available nowadays to help with the different strategies used in the disciplining of our children, and if used consistently, can be quite effective. I have researched different online resources and have spoken with numerous other parents and grandparents.

I have implemented many of these strategies with the rearing of my own children and grandchildren.

The most influential and effective strategy I have found is the use of the guidance of the Holy Bible and the Holy

Spirit, along with these alternative discipline strategies.

I cannot describe the weight, the guilt and shame, which was lifted off me when God showed me a better way to discipline my children. Spanking, whipping, slapping, yelling, cursing, swearing and other forms of physical and verbal punishment do not work long-lastingly to correct a child's behavior. By the way, correction and training are the ultimate purposes of discipline.

Verbal and physical punishment can cause long lasting physical, spiritual, mental, emotional, and psychological health issues, I can assure you that I know this personally.

This kind of punishment reinforces bad behavior and increases anger in a child. Even though your intentions may have been well intended, it can produce the opposite effect desired.

The love and kindness that should be portrayed works wonders. However, abrupt, harsh punishment damages and deteriorates relationships.

Physical punishment and verbal abuse sends the wrong message. It teaches our children that hitting, and aggression are appropriate ways to resolve conflict and vent frustration. It tells a child that someone that hits you can still love you. Whipping can send a highly confusing message.

I learned and used more positive and responsible parenting strategies. Here are a few things that have worked for me; but I will confess that it did not happen overnight for me and will not be an overnight accomplishment for you either. Many prayers went up, many tears I shed as I was learning, and it required a lot of willpower, self-control, love, patience, and long-suffering. Just what Dr. God ordered.

1 - Warning:

Warning comes before destruction. A parent should never punish their child for actions they didn't know were wrong, or rules that have not been established. Instead, give them a warning, show mercy, use the moment as a teaching moment. Now is the time to set clear protocols for the future. Be sure that they understand what acceptable behavior is and what is unacceptable behavior and the consequences for both. Consequences can be good or bad.

2 - Establish What is Right and what is Wrong:

Establish what are considered appropriate behaviors and inappropriate behaviors. Explaining why something should be done or why it should not be done can be helpful to a child's understanding. Instead of just saying 'because I said so.' Instill a moral compass within your child's consciousness. The Bible is a great guide and point of reference. The Ten Commandments are a very good starting point.

3 - Establish Consequences:

Give clear, concise rules that your children can follow and be consistent. Be sure to explain these rules in age-appropriate terms so that they can understand. Calmly and firmly explain the consequences if the rules are not followed. If the child is old enough, have them repeat back to you what has been said to ensure there is a clear understanding of what is to happen if the rules are not followed. Once established, let them make their own choices and do not be overbearing. Remember, never take away something your child truly needs, such as a meal. Consequences can encourage your child to make wiser decisions next time.

4 - Be Authoritative:
Display both love and consistency. An authoritative parent will establish clear boundaries and set high expectations for their child. This is not a time to debate, say what you mean and mean what you say. The authoritative parent will validate the child's feelings and offer comfort while using a firm tone, maintain a positive demeanor, while still expecting acceptable behavior.

5 - Model Desired Behaviors:
'Don't fight fire with fire.' Display the behavior you would like to see in your

children. You can't correct bad behavior with bad behavior. If your child is having a tantrum the parent cannot solve it by having one as well. For example: If they hit their siblings, hitting them is doing the exact thing you are trying to discipline them for. If a child is yelling, trying to over yell them will not help the situation. Can you recall that old saying: 'Do what I say, and not what I do'? This way of training will not correct bad behavior. 'Actions speak louder than words.' Take a deep breath and correct them with a calm, loving voice. A parent may need a timeout themselves.

6 - Don't Be A Hypocrite:

Why should you punish a child for things that they see you doing? This creates mixed feelings of anger and frustration. Just because you are bigger and in a position of power does not exempt you from your responsibility of demonstrating the behavior you should be trying to convey. If you swear and smoke in front of your child, why would you punish them for swearing and smoking? If you lie to your child or in front of your child, why do they get punished for lying? If you hit your child or anyone else in front of your child, why should they be punished for something they have learned from you?

7 - Keep Your Word:

If you tell your child that you are going to do something, whether it is a reward or a punishment, you must follow through with it. No idle threats. Don't make a promise you can't keep. By not keeping your word you are sending the message that lying is ok and you can expect that some trust will be lost.

8- Spend Quality Time:

Powerful tools for effective discipline are giving your children attention, spending quality time with them, getting to know them and them getting to know you. Just have fun together. Creating positive experiences that will reinforce good behaviors and discourage others. Making games out of tasks or turning them into challenges can be a fun way to accomplish a task. Verbal praise may be all the reward that is needed.

9 - Don't Feed The Beast:

Sometimes children can display selfish behavior and become attention seekers. Ignoring bad behavior can be an effective form of discipline as long as your child isn't doing something dangerous and gets plenty of attention for good behavior. Ignoring bad behavior can be an effective way of correcting it.

10 - Praise In Advance:

Help set the atmosphere with positive reinforcement and incentives. When giving demands, using encouraging and motivating word choices along with commands can be highly effective, especially early in the morning. For example: if you are trying to get a child to wake up and to get dressed for school, instead of saying wake-up and put your clothes on, you may say, good morning my sweet girl or boy, let's wake up and make mommy proud by getting yourself dressed this morning. Your child will most likely respond to your positive attitude with a positive attitude.

Words of praise are powerful, every time my aunt Lizzie Mae would see me, she would say: "I'm depending on you". Her affirming words and the words of all my other aunties, even to this day, encourage me to do right when I would think of doing wrong.

11 - Reward Good Behavior:

Praising and rewarding your child will reinforce good behavior and positive actions. Showing them kindness, compassion and enthusiasm builds self-esteem and motivates continued good behavior. Positive reinforcement can go a long way. Children need to know when they do something good as well as bad. Try to focus more on the good behavior; point it out and reward them for it.

12 - Hear Them Out:

Good listening and communication skills are important. Don't overreact or over criticize. Your child may have a good explanation for what they may or may not have done. Your child may have believed that they were doing something good. For example, they may have put water all over the floor thinking they were cleaning it. Ask the child why he or she is behaving in such a way. Let your child tell their side of the story before helping to solve the problem. Talk with your child about this rather than just giving consequences. Be sure that they hear you out. You have the final say.

13 - Plan Ahead:
Kids will be kids. Acknowledging that fact, you should plan in advance for their misbehavior, and how you will handle it when it occurs. They are still learning. Prepare the child for upcoming activities and how you expect them to behave and the consequences to follow if they misbehave. Be sure to always supervise small children. Try to prevent problems before they happen, like removing fragile and harmful things out of small children's reach. Make sure they have had enough rest, food, and activities. Look for teaching moments to practice discipline techniques ahead of time.

14 - Redirection:

Children sometimes misbehave because they are bored. Find some activities for your child to keep them engaged. If you are cleaning, let them help you with the process or give them a task as most kids enjoy participating. Yes, it may be quicker if you did it yourself, but this will be much more beneficial to both of you. Keeping a child focused on what they should be doing or how they should be conducting themselves will discourage other unwanted behaviors.

15 - A Time-out:

A time-out can help in teaching a child self-management and self-control, it allows the child to reflect on their unacceptable behavior.

Keep in mind that isolationism can be a reward for some children. Sending a child to their room is not the right strategy for every child. Having them sit or stand in your presence for an allotted amount of time after good behavior occurs may be more beneficial for some children. When giving the child a command, be sure to use a calm tone, clear instructions, with as little emotion as possible. This strategy works best by warning children that they will get a time out if they don't stop the unacceptable behavior. Remind them of what they did wrong in a few words. A time out also gives a parent time to take a deep breath and regroup.

16 - Suggestive Consequences:
Consequences like taking away privileges such as: phones, games, and other electronics, limiting TV time, restricting friends' visits, outdoor play time, driving privileges, going to social events, and increased chores can prove effective. Have them explain or write an essay on what they did wrong and what they could do better next time. Facing the music of their own choices and actions can eventually affect how they make future decisions of behavior.

17 - Do's and Don'ts.
Every child is different and unique. What works with one may not work with another. Don't discuss your children's

misbehavior with others in the presence of your children. Never use FEAR as a parenting tool. Don't show favoritism. Do not argue, fuss, or fight in the presence of the children at any time. Do not be judgmental, or condescending, remembering that we also once walked in their shoes. Be approachable and understanding. We do not have to be a super-parent; our children should know that we are not perfect. Sharing your own experiences and mistakes at an appropriate time can make a parent more relatable.

18 - Self Defense:
I believe there is a time and place for everything and hitting a child as a punishment is not one of them. Some parents believe that aggressive physical punishment helps prepare a child for a world that is not always so nice. Some parents believe that slapping a child around teaches a child survival skill, how to be tough, to take a punch, and to defend themselves. This form of teaching can be unhealthy for the child, as well as for the parent-child

relationship. As a result, this method could cause anger and resentment. The child is likely to become an aggressor, or a bully. If a parent wants to teach a child to defend themselves, they should research and perhaps enroll their child in an age-appropriate self-defense class that teaches discipline and self-control. If a parent prefers to teach their child themselves, the parent should educate themselves on the subject matter first, then teach their child at a time that is specifically geared for that training and not as a punishment.

19 - Use Wisdom:

Remember that disciplining, as opposed to punishing, focuses on training, instructing, informing, correcting, and teaching our children to behave instead of just punishing them for misbehaving. Punishment may relieve your stress level but will not produce the desired result in the child's behavior.
When considering an appropriate discipline strategy, choose a method that will help you achieve your behavioral objectives.

Hopefully, by now the veil is beginning to be lifted from your eyes as to why I write. Even though I discourage physical punishment, it doesn't mean I discourage discipline. In fact, safe and effective discipline is a must.

A better way may be right in your grasp. Let's begin again by using a more positive approach to discipline, with plenty of love, patience, prayer, and faith.

Please understand, parents are human, we too are constantly learning, and we do not always get it right, no matter how hard we try. Parents do not beat yourselves up about how you have possibly done disciplining wrong in the past. Forgive yourself, dust yourself off, apologize to God and to your child, if *possible. You may never realize how important and powerful an apology can be. Learn from your mistakes and try* again. Mistakes sometimes are our best teachers.

'Brethren, if a man be overtaken in a fault, ye which are spiritual, restore such an one in the spirit of meekness; considering thyself, lest thou also be tempted.' Galatians 6:1 KJV

A Better Way

The Power of the Tongue

Believe it or not, one of the strongest weapons that we possess is our tongue. The words of our mouth are powerful! They can be used as a deadly poison, or as deadly as throwing stones. Words can cut like a knife.

Our words can also be medicine to the sick, healing to the broken, and life to the dying spirit. People often overlook the power of the tongue. When choosing our words we should choose them wisely, and wisdom comes from God. The tongue can be used to take away life, just as quickly as it can be used to speak life.

The tongue can be used to tear one's spirit down, just as easily as it can help to lift one's spirit up.

'But no man can tame the tongue. It is an unruly evil, full of deadly poison.'
James 3:8 NKJV

Do you recall that old saying, 'sticks and stones may break my bones, but words will never hurt me'? Words absolutely do hurt. What we say matters as well as how we say it. Especially when it comes from someone that we love and trust while they supposedly love us.

Parents are their child's most influential role model. If you lose your cool and act aggressively when challenging situations present themselves, whether that moment is with your spouse, a family member, your child or the mailman, you will likely raise a child who does the same.

'Death and life are in the power of the tongue, And those who love it will eat its fruit.' Proverbs 18:21 NKJV

Words used to threaten, to belittle, to instill fear, to gain or maintain power and control over someone is verbal abuse. Verbal abuse may not involve physical contact, but it can still be extremely harmful and may cause emotional, spiritual, and psychological damage.

In the heat of the moment, parents may say things intentionally or unintentionally that they may later regret, such as: threats of causing bodily harm to their children, things like: 'I'll beat you into next week.' 'I'm going to beat the black off of you.' I am going to slap the mess out of you.' 'I will beat some sense into you.' 'I brought you into this world, I will take you out.'

This is definitely verbal abuse and wrath. When you say these kinds of things to your child, whether you intend to act on it or not, they are still very serious threats. Like any threat it puts a child in an uneasy state of mind and over time can lead to fear and a lack of trust. Unfortunately, it is not hard to understand why as their children get older. Some parents must sleep with one eye open, always on the alert as a result of their previous actions with their children.

There are many other forms of verbal abuse that are just as harmful. These include rejection, demeaning remarks, name-calling, (whether they are direct or indirect) and negative criticism. Also, saying things like, 'you can't do anything right.' 'you're good for nothing,' 'you will never amount to nothing.' or calling your child stupid, lazy, or fat. Do not mock your child to their face or to someone else where the child can hear you. Saying things like 'they're dumber than a bag of rocks,' 'or they are not the brightest crayon in the box.' Also, threatening your child with abandonment. Saying things like, 'I wish you'd never been born,' 'I should have given you up for adoption,' 'I wish I had gotten an abortion, or even blaming a child for making a parent's life harder or miserable.

Being on the receiving end of verbal abuse of any kind can cause an individual to question their own intelligence, value, and self-worth. Verbal abuse may cause a child to develop anxiety. A child may become anti-social, depressed and self-destructive later in life. They may use drugs and alcohol as a coping mechanism, or even becoming a menace to society in response to all the negativity that occurred in their lives, through no fault of their own initially. They may become the abuser later in life as a result of being abused.

They may remain in an abusive relationship because they may believe that abuse is an expression of love. They may act out by inflicting physical harm to themselves such as scratching and cutting and even attempting or committing suicide or reflect pain out on others.

Verbal punishment is just as toxic as physical punishment. Leaving behind invisible scars. As a child, and even now as an adult, when people say harsh things or yell at me, in some instances, it gives me anxiety. So, for the most part, I have learned to tune out the noise to protect myself. However, sometimes that even gets hard to do.

I remember a time that I must have frustrated my mother so badly that out of her aggravation she asked me two very disturbing questions: "Why did I have to be so different"? "Why couldn't I be more like my sisters"? I believe that she was thinking out loud. I did not know how to respond. Those questions played

back in my head over and over again
leading me to think that there was
something wrong with me, and that my
sisters were better than me.

Eventually, I came to understand
that different doesn't mean bad. Yes, I
may not be like my other sisters in many
ways, but God doesn't love me any less
and neither did my parents.

Even though my sisters and I lived
in the same house, we were raised by
the same parents, and we believed in
the same God, my parents' discipline
methods affected me much differently,
and my views on discipline are not the
same. Positive reinforcement and
incentives were more effective with me,
rather than harsh punishment. I believe
it was because in my heart, I really have
always wanted to do the right things and
to please God as well as my parents.

One of the differences between
my sisters and me is that I can handle
physical pain a lot better than emotional
pain. I guess you can say that I am
tough on the outside but soft on the
inside. For me, even though spanking
may have been an outward event, it

affected me more inwardly. Actions speak louder than words and harsh words are just as painful as physical punishment.

So, I am different and there is nothing wrong with that. Seeing myself how God sees me and not how man sees me is something I am still learning to embrace.

One of the biggest dilemmas with abuse is that God has meticulously designed the human body to pay closer attention to potentially dangerous threats, whether the threats are verbal or physical. Remembering pain and danger are the body's way of trying to protect itself.

Studies show that people tend to recall negative memories quicker than positive ones. Which means, a few positive comments may not offset one negative comment. Therefore, when you can have one parent using positive words and the other using negative words, unfortunately the potential for damage is still present. The consequences may be apparent for years to come.

The use of positive affirmations can be a powerful and effective tool for ourselves as well as for our children. Affirmations train or retrain the brain to develop a belief about oneself. Using positive words while looking in a mirror should be done every day to be most effective.

The Bible has plenty of powerful affirmations within it. These affirmations are the most powerful because they help us to focus and rely on the God qualities that He has deposited within us and not relying on our own strength.

Positive Affirmations:
- I am beautiful
- I am smart
- I am chosen
- I am forgiven
- I am loved
- I am free
- I am obedient
- I am the head and not the tail
- I am above and not beneath
- I can do all things through Christ Who strengthens me
- I am blessed and highly favored

- I am fearfully and wonderfully made
- I will not grow weary in doing good
- I will not fear, for God is always with me
- I will believe and trust in God
- I have the mind of Christ
- I will have a good day
- I will be the best that I can be
- I am not perfect, and that's ok
- I will be kind to others
- I will have a positive attitude
- I will be a light for others
- My past doesn't define me

The tongue is a powerful tool, an instrument that can be used for good or for evil. This old saying stands true and has excellent value today, 'If you can't say something nice then, don't say anything at all.' A parent's words should be ones of love, that uplift, encourage, motivate, and edify for correction and instruction. In moments of stress, frustration, and anger, try to refrain from saying anything harsh to your child. Even if that means you may need to give **yourself** a timeout. Take a deep breath and ask God to help you in your moments of weakness, yes, we all have them.

'Behold, they belch out with their mouth: Swords are in their lips: For who, say they, doth hear?' Psalm 59:7 KJV

Do not let your mouth cause your flesh to sin, nor say before the messenger of God that it was an error. Why should God be angry at your excuse and destroy the work of your hands?
Ecclesiastes 5:6 NKJV

'A fool's mouth is his destruction, And his lips are the snare of his soul.' Proverbs 18:7 KJV

'But no man can tame the tongue. It is an unruly evil, full of deadly poison. With it we bless our God and Father, and with it we curse men, who have been made in the similitude of God. Out of the same mouth proceed blessing and cursing. My brethren, these things ought not to be so. ' James 3:8-10 NKJV

There are many other resources available today that you can also use. (See: References and Resources)

Violence Begets Violence

Violence is emotionally (fleshly) motivated. The higher and more intense the emotions run, the higher the risk of violent behavior. Violence is a behavior involving physical force intended to hurt, damage, or kill someone or something.

As parents, we are our children's role models. They learn to mimic our behavior at a very early age. Everything we say and do influences our children's personalities, character, choices, and actions, one way or another.

'Let no one despise your youth, but be an example to the believers in word, in conduct, in love, in spirit, in faith, in purity.'
I Timothy 4:12 NKJV

The way we handle various situations plays a huge role in how they will handle similar situations in their future. For example: If Mary hits John, then you discipline Mary by hitting Mary, this only reinforces Mary's action, and validates violent behavior for both children. If physical punishment is intended to inflict pain in order to teach a lesson; then what is the lesson you're teaching them? Is the lesson that it's acceptable to hit someone when you are mad or unhappy with someone's behavior?

'Repay no one evil for evil. Have regard for good things in the sight of all men. If it is possible, as much as depends on you, live peaceably with all men. '
Romans 12:17-18 NKJV

Food For Thought:
In what capacity of today's society is it acceptable for a person to use the lessons taught by aggressive physical punishment?

Maybe, if a person is considering living the life of a gangster, which would bring its own repercussions; or perhaps if an individual is engaging or pursuing a career in professional boxing. There are still guidelines that govern boxing that include training and regulations; not just randomly hitting another person.

Due to my newly found convictions, I am not so sure God would be pleased with that either, but that's a topic for another time.

I remember, as if it was yesterday, the first time that I popped my daughter on the hand. She was just learning to walk. We were at my parent's home. Man did my mother have a lot of nice figurines and whatnots all throughout the house; everything was neat and orderly. You would not have guessed by looking around the home that she ran a small home daycare. My mother did not believe in moving things out of the reach of children. She believed that children should be taught not to touch her nice things.

One day my precious little baby girl had pulled herself up to the coffee table and began walking around it. I was so proud of her. And as you can probably imagine, something caught my daughter's eye and she attempted to touch it. So, I told my little girl "no no" and then I popped her hand just as I had seen my mother do on several occasions to other children. What happened next shocked me. My little girl, who could barely walk, paused and looked at me with a face of confusion and disbelief that I will never forget. As she continued walking around the table again, the same whatnot caught her attention. She reached for it again, so I told her "no no" with a firmer tone, then I popped her hand a little harder. She paused and looked at me in shock with her lip poked out and whimpered just a bit. Then to my surprise she made the hand gesture as if she was popping me back.

It was then that I realized that hitting is a taught and learned behavior. Unfortunately, I was the teacher.

Which leads me to the question, why do we do it? Why do we yell and curse, hit, spank, whip, slap, paddle and beat our children? After much thought, the conclusion that I have reached is this. Many people all over the world use physical punishment because they *BELIEVE* that it is the right thing to do, and/or they believe that it works. There are many factors over time that may have influenced these beliefs.

People sometimes develop the herd-mentality, following the crowd.

A parent's own childhood experiences can normalize physical punishment. For many parents, whipping and spanking as a punishment is a natural form of discipline that exerts the parent's authority. It is possible they were spanked as a child themselves. A parent may have tried spanking as a form of punishment which, for a short time, seems to have worked, until they have to do it again and again, and sometimes with more intensity. Some parents whip their children because they get aggravated, overwhelmed, or just downright mad. Whipping may be a response to a child's misbehavior and the parent may just react because they don't know what else to do. A parent's religious beliefs, ethnic or racial connection, counselors, advisors, pastors, socio-economic status, a parent's education level, as well as stress levels are all influential factors.

As an African American parent, I have been influenced by most-if not all of these factors. My previous perceptions were deeply rooted in these practices for disciplining my children. Initially, I blamed my outlook on whipping my children as a disciplinary measure taught by my religious background in a Pentecostal Church, The Church of God in Christ (COGIC), who relentlessly preached *"spare the rod, spoil the child"*. Later I realized that for me, the root of the matter ran much deeper than religion. Even deeper than I can comprehend and possibly deeper than I can truly explain.

God revealed to me that physical punishment extended to a time even before the era of Moses where there was NO law or order. Moses was given the law, and order was established by way of the Ten Commandments in the Old Testament.

Depending on the timeline of the Bible you are reading, the world was an extremely violent place. Living under the law the order of the day was 'an eye for an eye', if you "lived by the sword you died by the sword; 'kill or be killed'. If you committed a crime, you could have been stoned to death. Before the era of Moses, people were ruled by their own conscience, or lack of conscience (no law) which was not a good thing either. Slavery is a prime example of the consciousness of man, or should I say the lack there of.

'For I know that in me (that is, in my flesh,) dwelleth no good thing: for to will is present with me; but how to perform that which is good I find not.'
Romans 7:18 KJV

Slavery is not a black or a white thing. Slavery is a crime against humanity as it has been present throughout the world and throughout time. For thousands of years, slavery was an acceptable way of life. Slavery was a legal institution in which a person (the slave) was the property of another (the master). Slavery dates to ancient times. Slaves endured all types of abuse, including verbal abuse, as they were called everything but a child of God.

Slaves were punished by whippings, shackling, hangings, beatings, burnings, mutilation, branding, raped, dismembered, imprisonment, tortured, and sold like livestock from one slave master to another. These brutal methods of punishment were used to dishearten, to control and to instill fear into their slaves. It was used to force submission, and often given out in response to disobedience or perceived infractions, but sometimes abuse was performed to re-assert the dominance of the master (or overseer) over the slave. Pregnant women and children were not exempt from these cruel and inhumane disciplinary/abusive methods.

Unfortunately, even though we have come away from blatant open slavery, human exploitation still exists today, in one form or another. It may not be as prevalent as it used to be, but it still exists in many places in our world.

Even though we may have survived the slavery of earlier times, we are left with a legacy of psychological slavery that we see in many homes, churches, and hear of in society today.

These psychological slavery effects are more prevalent in homes where harsh verbal and physical punishment is, and where highly abusive relationships exist. Many times, this tend to lead to highly violent crimes.

Corporal punishment is one of the lingering remnants of slavery. It is a disciplinary method in which a supervising adult deliberately inflicts pain upon another person/a child, in response to a child's unacceptable behavior. Schools are one of the last public institutions where corporal punishment is still legal. It is permitted in Nineteen (19) states out of the fifty (50) states in the United States of America. It is much more widespread across schools in some states, particularly Alabama, Mississippi, and Arkansas where half of all students attend schools that still use corporal punishment.

Study after study concludes that abused children and adults are more likely to become abusers themselves, resulting in a vicious cycle of abuse.

Physical discipline is an unhealthy cycle that is psychologically embedded into our homes, schools, churches, governments, and society today. It's important to understand that spanking, whipping, cursing, yelling, and physical punishment to any degree can often escalate a child's bad behavior. On one end of the scale abuse can motivate a child to fight back or take their anger out on others, (the abuser). On the other end the abused may learn how to endure the pain; they may become timid and fearful therefore are more likely to be abused further. A child's tolerance to pain may increase. Therefore, the intensity of the abuse may increase for its desired effectiveness. Either way the cycle continues. I was hit so I hit, the more I hit the more I get hit, and the more likely this same behavior is demonstrated throughout life and is passed onto their children, and onto their children's children for generations to come.

Toxic and barbaric behavior patterns that I believe were derived from slavery and the government, are extending to our schools, our homes, our churches and is spilling over into the communities.

Society today is full of increasing violence, lawlessness, mass shootings, drug crimes, mental health related crimes, police brutality, human trafficking, domestic abuse, social media bullying, as well as displaying violent games, movies, and TV shows.

Numerous people, especially church folks, believe that much of this is occurring because parents are not whipping their children as much as they used to. Governmental agencies have established laws that discourage physical punishment and abuse, which are designed to protect our children.

However, I believe that society's moral decline is directly related to the lack of proper child discipline, the lack of proper teaching and correction. I believe society's moral decline is not caused by the decrease of physical punishment, but rather the lack of healthy discipline, the lack of parents leading by example and living a God-led life and displaying Godly love.

In order to correct our children's behavior, we may first need to correct our own.

'See that none render evil for evil unto any man; but ever follow that which is good, both among yourselves, and to all men.'
1 Thessalonians 5:15 KJV

There are essential principles that we are neglecting to apply to every area of our life including the area of child discipline. The principles of sowing and reaping. We harvest only what we plant. If you sow seeds of hate, anger, strife and violence, we will reap hate, anger, strife and violence. If we plant seeds of love, happiness, peace, and kindness, we will harvest love, happiness, peace, and kindness. This principle holds true whether we believe it or not.

'Be not deceived; God is not mocked: for whatsoever a man sow shall he also reap. For he that soweth to his flesh shall of the flesh reap corruption; but he that soweth to the Spirit shall of the Spirit reap life everlasting.'
Galatians 6:7-8 KJV

It is frightening to see that society is becoming more consciously aware of the dangers of corporal punishment and physical assault than the church.

Physical punishment is not the answer to the problem, but it is the problem itself. There are laws in place to guard against child abuse and with good reason. The world, as well as church folks alike have abused their authority long enough.

The Rod of Correction

The Supreme Court ruled that state mandated class prayers in public schools were unconstitutional in the landmark case of Engle vs. Vital in June 1962. The problem with separation of church and state is that God originally established government!

Our school systems have taken a turn for the worst since the removal of the Ten Commandments and since they removed prayer from schools. In fact, I believe that the situation has gotten much worse. The school was where many of our children learned Biblical values and morals, regardless of whether or not they were affiliated with a church, and whether or not they were taught at home. Although the home used to be and should still be the primary place that they are taught, the principles were reinforced at school before the ruling in 1962.

In many homes today, parents are disciplining their children very little, too much or not at all.

This younger generation have become so self-centered, they feel it's all about me-me-me and my wants and needs. Single parent homes are at an all-time high these days. If a child is blessed enough to have both parents in the home, one or both parents are working outside of the home. Which means in many cases, they may be spending more time away from their children than with them. This leaves it up to someone else to teach their children.

When some parents are with their children, they are still not present. They are too exhausted from working or doing other extracurricular activities to barely feed and clothe their children; so truly disciplining them is quickly becoming a thing of the past.

Many parents nowadays are more interested in going out for a night on the town and enjoying their lives, rather than teaching their children. Many parents try to be their children's friend instead of an authority figure.

A lot of parents nowadays are less engaged with their children. Instead, they are letting electronic devices and social media teach their children. More parents and their children are attending church much less than they did years ago. Also, when the parents do happen to take their children to church, there are lots of times that the preacher is not preaching age-appropriate material for a child's understanding.

Yes, removing prayer out of school may not have been the brightest idea; however, just because prayer was removed from school does not relieve parents of our obligation to teach our children to keep a prayer in their hearts, to teach them the Word of God and the love and respect for the Lord. Our children need both a school education and Jesus, the ROC, the Living Word of God.

The removal of the Ten Commandments and prayer from school has had a direct impact on our society today. Nevertheless, many parents are neglecting to teach children important life principles at home, and this has an even greater negative impact in all of our lives. Also, some results of the lack of teaching our children the Ten Commandments and failing to pray with them regularly leaves them vulnerable to being influenced by others that do not share our values.

1. You shall have no other gods before Me.

Church attendance continues to decline. People are into horoscopes, witchcraft, and communicating with the dead. People choose sports and extracurricular activities over church attendance. People are allowing drug addictions, pornography, other addictions, and impurities to rule their lives and become their god.

2. You shall not make idols.

Money, houses, cars, sports figures, movie stars, musical artists and the rich and famous, as well as pride in themselves, are held more highly esteemed than God.

3. You shall not take the Name of the Lord your God in vain.

People use God's name so loosely, God said this, and God said that. Foul language is allowed on television, radio, and movies misusing His Name. The youth embrace swearing in music and their daily speaking because they were not taught to honor God.

4. Remember the Sabbath day, to keep it Holy.

The love of money is driving businesses to stay open every day of the week and people are choosing to work rather than to attend church and rest on that day. Sporting events, games, movies, and other activities are keeping people too busy to rest and reflect on how good God is.

5. Honor your father and your mother.

Children do not respect mothers and fathers like they should. Many parents are not earning the respect of their children because of the lifestyles that they choose to live. Many women are raising their children without a father. Child and elderly abuse and neglect are increasing. Families are more diverse these days, but they struggle to be accepted.

6. You shall not murder.
Violent crime rates are unbelievable.
Gun crimes are increasing by the day.
Mass murders are happening much
more frequently. Youths are bringing
guns and knives to school with the intent
to kill people who have offended them.
Teen suicide is at an all-time high.
Television, movies, and video games
have glamorized guns, violence and
killing, resulting in desensitization in our
children's moral compass. Police
brutality is steadily rising. The lack of
respect for a person's life as God's
creation is blatantly apparent. Children
are killing each other's spirit through
bullying, and verbal abuse.

7. You shall not commit adultery.
The divorce rate has gone through the
roof, even in Christian communities.
Families are being torn apart by people
who lack honor in their commitment and
self-control is non-existent in many
marital relationships. Domestic violence
is on the rise. Same-sex families,
transgender families, and single-parent
homes are increasing at alarming rates.

Human trafficking and prostitution has skyrocketed too.

8. You shall not steal.

Children and adults alike have no respect for other people's belongings. When they see something, they want, they take it instead of working for it, with little or no remorse for the pain that they cause someone else to suffer at the loss.

9. You shall not bear false witness against your neighbor.

Gossiping has become the new pass-time as we see on many of the TV talk shows. Our nation leaders demonstrate that lying is acceptable when it suits their purpose. We tarnish one another's character with little thought to the damage it does to others.

10. You shall not covet.

Many people in our society want to keep up with the Joneses. They are jealous of their neighbor's home, vehicle, clothes, and private school. They live beyond their means so that they can look good in church, at work and in their community. They are backstabbing people on their jobs to make themselves look good, to get a promotion, to get someone else's position on the job, or to feel superior.

Teaching our children, the Ten Commandments out of the Old Testament is extremely beneficial. However, depending on the age of a child, the golden rule may be a better place to start. 'Do unto others, like you want them to do unto you.' However, that is only the beginning. Jesus is the "ROC", The Living Word of God, which is the rod and a sword that Jesus expects parents to use as instruments for the correction and reproof and disciplining (training) of His little disciples. As a child grows, so should their understanding, knowledge, wisdom, love and respect for God and others.

Children are our future, and what we teach our children today has a direct impact on what society will look like tomorrow.

Therefore, we should also teach our children the New Testament as well as the Old Testament. If we are to teach our children to treat others the way, they want others to treat them. Why don't we treat our children in the way we want to be treated? We must teach by example which is the way Jesus lived His life here on earth. Jesus told us to do away with all wrath, bitterness, anger and strife and to put on the fruit of the spirit.

'But if you are led by the Spirit, you are not under the law.'
Galatians 5:18 NKJV

'Now the works of the flesh are evident, which are: adultery, fornication, uncleanness, lewdness, idolatry, sorcery, hatred, contentions, jealousies, outbursts of wrath, selfish ambitions, dissensions, heresies, envy, murders, drunkenness, revelries, and the like; of which I tell you beforehand, just as I also told you in time past, that those who practice such things will not inherit the kingdom of God. But the fruit of the Spirit is love, joy, peace, longsuffering, kindness, goodness, faithfulness, gentleness, self-control. Against such there is no law. ' Galatians 5:19-23 NKJV

Unfortunately, there are many Christians who are stuck in the teaching of the law and traditions. They still believe that God literally wants parents to "BEAT" God's little disciples with their hands or with some man-made object as a form of discipline to make them submit, honor, and obey a parent's authority, and to save their souls from hell.

These barbaric concepts and violent conditionings completely contradict the way Jesus Christ is teaching us to live today.

'And do not be conformed to this world, but be transformed by the renewing of your mind, that you may prove what is that good and acceptable and perfect will of God.'
Romans 12:2 NKJV

The Scribes and the Pharisees used Scriptures out of context just the way some church folks do today. Church folks, even back in Jesus' time on earth, considered Jesus to be very controversial when He came on the scene. Jesus was teaching the message of salvation, the message of love, peace, grace and mercy. Jesus was showing the people a better way to achieve the same goal. However, many times the message fell on deaf ears and blind eyes.

Most people don't like change. People tend to get stuck in a particular era of time, traditions, or what they are familiar and comfortable with. However, over the passing of time people do change. God is God and God will be God whether we believe Him or not. God doesn't change but people do change. God doesn't change but His methods do. Jesus is God's Agent of change for mankind. Through Jesus, we have the power within us to change.

The "ROC", the **R**od **O**f **C**orrection is a spiritual weapon, which is the Bible and the Living Word of God. Christ Jesus and the Holy Spirit are our spiritual weapons we must use to achieve our victories. We are in spiritual warfare on a daily basis. In order to win this fight, we must use the spiritual weapons that God has provided for us and not our own limited knowledge.

'For we wrestle not against flesh and blood, but against principalities, against powers, against the rulers of the darkness of this world, against spiritual wickedness in high places.'
Ephesians 6:12 KJV

'He who spares the rod hates his son, but he who loves him is careful to discipline him. '
Proverbs 13:24 KJV

"Spare The Rod, Spoil The Child"

This is a quote that many people use referring to the Scriptures that we should consider looking at from a different perspective. Is it possible that we have been looking at this Scripture through our earthly lens, and not the spiritual lens in the way in which it was intended? Ask yourself what would Jesus Christ say about it?

'Saying, "Do not touch My anointed ones, And do My prophets no harm." '
I Chronicles 16:22 NKJV

I believe Christ would say something like: Follow peace with all mankind, love covers a multitude of faults, I am the Way, the "ROC", the True and Living Word. Do not withhold instruction and discipline but teach them the way of the Lord. Believe in me, whether you plant or water, I will give the increase. Vengeance belongs to me. Whatever is right I will pay.

122

'Let no one despise your youth, but be an example to the believers in word, in conduct, in love, in spirit, in faith, in purity. '
I Timothy 4:12 NKJV

It is absolutely essential to teach our children about Christ, and the Word of God. Nevertheless, the Word of God is not only for our children but also for ourselves. We are all judged by the Word, we live or die by the Word, the "ROC."

When we discipline and correct our children, we need to be very sure that our heart is right, and our flesh is in check.

Sometimes we have to pray. Take a pause, and just wait on the Lord for a bit. Be still and know that God is God. Waiting while expecting Him to give us wisdom and instruction on what to do and how to do it.

We need to be sure that we are acting out of the spirit of love and in a way that is pleasing to God.

New Testament Teaching:

'Let them alone. They are blind leaders of the blind. And if the blind leads the blind, both will fall into a ditch.'
Matthew 15:14 NKJV

'Whoever receives one little child like this in My name receives Me. "Whoever causes one of these little ones who believe in Me to sin, it would be better for him if a millstone were hung around his neck, and he were drowned in the depth of the sea. Woe to the world because of offenses! For offenses must come, but woe to that man by whom the offense comes!'
Matthew 18:5-7 NKJV

'And Jesus answered him, The first of all the commandments is, Hear, O Israel; The Lord our God is one Lord:'
Mark 12:29 KJV

'and thou shalt love the Lord thy God with all thy heart, and with all thy soul, and with all thy mind, and with all thy strength: this is the first commandment.'
Mark 12:30 KJV

'And the second is like, namely this, Thou shalt love thy neighbour as thyself. There is none other commandment greater than these.'
Mark 12:31 KJV

'There is no fear in love; but perfect love casteth out fear: because fear hath torment. He that feareth is not made perfect in love.'
1 John 4:18 KJV

'Owe no man anything, but to love one another: for he that loveth another hath fulfilled the law. For this, Thou shalt not commit adultery, Thou shalt not kill, Thou shalt not steal, Thou shalt not bear false witness, Thou shalt not covet; and if there be any other commandment, it is briefly comprehended in this saying, namely, Thou shalt love thy neighbour as thyself. Love worketh no ill to his neighbour: therefore love is the fulfilling of the law. And that, knowing the time, that now it is high time to awake out of sleep: for now is our salvation nearer than when we believed.'
Romans 13: 8-11 KJV

'If My people who are called by My name will humble themselves, and pray and seek My face, and turn from their wicked ways, then I will hear from heaven, and will forgive their sin and heal their land.'
II Chronicles 7:14 NKJV

A Wake-up Call

After working on my book for about two months, I had a dream. I dreamed that I was a teacher's assistant in a classroom. One day the teacher and I began to pass back drawings that the students had drawn, and the teacher had graded. It was then that a dark spirit appeared in the classroom.

The dark spirit was wearing a dusty-gray colored hooded robe. The teacher and I stopped passing out the drawings and watched the spirit as it slowly moved up and down the aisles. The dark spirit then jumped from one drawing to the next causing each child's soul to become limp. Within minutes the dark spirit flew away rejoicing with the children's limp souls.

Soon after, another spirit appeared in the classroom. It was a spirit of light. The spirit of light told me to tell all the children that remained in the classroom to ask the Lord to forgive them for their bad behaviors. In addition, he told me to do it quickly.

I obeyed the spirit of light and
stood in the middle of the classroom and
with a most urgent voice, I told every
child to ask the Lord for forgiveness of
all their misbehavior and to ask the Lord
to remove from their hearts anything
that is not pleasing to the Lord. The
children did just as I asked.

The teacher passed out the
remaining drawings. The dark spirit
returned to the classroom and stood
toward the back of the room. He leaned
his back against the wall with his arms
folded. He had one foot propped on the
wall behind him. The room began to fill
with his stench.

He watched the children, who
were unaware of the danger that
surrounded them, admire their work. He
looked at me and I looked at him. I
looked him straight in his fiery eyes and
I boldly said to him, "not this time". The
dark spirit laughed at me.

He then moved up and down the
aisle just as he had done before. The
teacher and I began to pray. He
searched and searched for drawings
that he could enter but there were none

this time. This made him angry, and the dark spirit began to mourn and groan.

He started to fly away when the spirit of light entered the room. The spirit of light demanded that the dark spirit release the souls which he had claimed earlier. The dark spirit had no choice but to let the souls go. The dark spirit mourned and flew away with great sorrow.

After waking up from this dream I laid across my bed in confusion and I asked the Lord to please give me the meaning of this dream if it was for me to know. The answer I got was this.

The classroom represents the home. The teacher represents the parent or guardian of the children. The teacher's assistant represents the parents' helper, a pastor, or someone in authority. The drawing represents the heart of the children, which is the door of the child's soul. The drawing in the hands of the teachers and the teacher's assistant represents that the heart of the children are in the hands of the parents, teachers, or an authority figure. The drawing in the hands of the child represents that the children's hearts are no longer in the hands of the authority, but that the children are now responsible for his or her own soul. The child holding and admiring their work, represented that the child was now faced with their own fate.

The dark spirit represents Satan or his evil demons. The spirit jumping in the child's picture represents an evil spirit entering a child's heart. The limp souls represent the weakness that comes with the presence of evil. The spirit flying around with the children's souls represents Satan's victory. He had claimed their souls as his own. The dark spirit rejoicing represents a prideful spirit, that was very glad about what he had accomplished.

The teacher and the assistant standing there watching represent idle-minded people, authority figures, which see ungodly things going on around them and do or say nothing about it.

There are people who do not help others that they see in need of help. Some parents turn a blind eye to the tactics that Satan uses against our children. The spirit of light that brings the message of repentance is the Holy Spirit. The message represents the Word of God, through Whom we receive our salvation. The timing of the spirit of light represents that God is in control, even when it may not look like it. The urgency in the teacher's assistance voice represents the critical need. It was a warning that there was no time to waste.

The children's prayers of repentance symbolizes there will come a time in every child's life that they must go to God for themselves. Passing the drawings on the second time represents the second chance in which God gives the parents and the parents' helpers, to supply their children with the tools needed to protect their souls against Satan. This tool is the Word of God.

The dark spirits standing toward the back of the room watching represent Satan's vanity and confidence in his abilities. He believes if he does it once, he can do it again.

On the second attempt, Satan tries and fails to regain more souls and becomes angry which representing that Satan no longer has access to the children's soul because after the Word of God came into their hearts. Sin had left their hearts and the door was now closed to Satan. The demand by the spirit of light for the spirit of darkness to release the souls he had taken represents the Devil is no match for God and the Devil does not have the final say. The mourning represents the disappointment of (his) Satan's defeat.

In other words, everyone needs to seek the Lord for themselves; we must keep God's Word in our hearts. In addition, parents and every child of God has the responsibility of helping others. We cannot sit around twiddling our thumbs hoping that Satan will just go away. Satan comes only to steal, kill, and destroy.

We have an obligation to teach God's Word to every man, woman, boy, or girl, because Satan does not care what age we are. All he cares about is winning our souls.

Those of us who are believers know that in the end Satan loses. In the meantime, let's not help Satan in the fight by fighting our children. Our fight is with the Devil. Let us give our children what they need to win. Let us teach our children to love God and hate the Devil. Remember, 'two wrongs do not make a right'. I say, A believer all day keeps the Devil away. A prayer all day keeps Satan at bay.

An Invitation To Christ:

'while it is said: "Today, if you will hear His voice, Do not harden your hearts as in the rebellion." ' Hebrews 3:15 NKJV

'From that time Jesus began to preach, and to say, Repent: for the kingdom of heaven is at hand. ' Matthew 4:17 KJV

'Verily I say unto you, Whosoever shall not receive the kingdom of God as a little child shall in no wise enter therein. '
Luke 18:17 KJV

'For God so loved the world, that he gave his only begotten Son, that whosoever believeth in him should not perish, but have everlasting life. For God sent not his Son into the world to

condemn the world; but that the world through him might be saved. ' John 3:16-17 KJV

'that if you confess with your mouth the Lord Jesus and believe in your heart that God has raised Him from the dead, you will be saved. For with the heart one believes unto righteousness, and with the mouth confession is made unto salvation. '
Romans 10:9-10 NKJV

The Lord's Prayer:
'In this manner, therefore, pray: Our Father in heaven, Hallowed be Your name. Your kingdom come. Your will be done On earth as it is in heaven. Give us this day our daily bread. And forgive us our debts, As we forgive our debtors. And do not lead us into temptation, But deliver us from the evil one. For Yours is the kingdom and the power and the glory forever. Amen.' Matthew 6:9-13 NKJV

Believers Believe

As believers, what we believe may not matter to others, but what we believe matters to God! In fact, our faith means everything to Him.

But without faith it is impossible to please Him, for he who comes to God must believe that He is, and that He is a rewarder of those who diligently seek Him. Hebrews 11:6 NKJV

By now the contents of this book may seem somewhat repetitive. However, it is intentional. It is in hope that the persistent reiteration will "BEAT" the message of love, not hate, peace not violence, teaching and correcting not harsh punishment, into the hearts and souls of the readers. As a teacher by trade, I know all too well that sometimes it takes repetition to truly grasp an idea or a concept.

A person's behavior will not change unless their beliefs change. Beliefs are formed over time and are influenced by many things. God knows that better than anyone because He made us. That is why He has instructed us not just to read His Word, but to study it, to meditate on it, to put it before us day and night.

'Therefore shall ye lay up these my words in your heart and in your soul, and bind them for a sign upon your hand, that they may be as frontlets between your eyes. And ye shall teach them your children, speaking of them when thou sittest in thine house, and when thou walkest by the way, when thou liest down, and when thou risest up. And thou shalt write them upon the door posts of thine house, and upon thy gates: ' Deuteronomy 11:18-20 NKJV

We must believe in God in all things, not just some things. We must trust His plan for our lives and our children's lives; that includes allowing The Holy Spirit to help us in the area for discipline of our children. God has left instructions, which is the Bible, His Holy Word. The Bible tells us to train a child up in the way that they should go. The Bible also says that the Lord will write His Word in our hearts. Jesus modeled the life in which we are to live, and He has sent a Comforter and a Counselor Who is the Holy Spirit, He will guide us in righteousness and in the way of truth.

All we have to do is study His Word, ask and believe.

'So then faith comes by hearing, and hearing by the word of God.'
Romans 10:17 NKJV

Knowing isn't believing and believing is not always trusting. You may know that God is God, the Creator of the universe, because that is what you have been told. You may believe that God had a Son named Jesus, who died on the cross for your transgressions and rose from the dead for our salvation and still decide not to trust Him to be Lord of your life. Howbeit, it becomes personal salvation to you when you believe the Truth of His Word and invite Him to be Savior and Lord of your personal life.

'Now faith is the substance of things hoped for, the evidence of things not seen.'
Hebrews 11:1 NKJV

Sometimes trusting means waiting on God, which in most cases takes a deeper level of faith and trust. People tend to take matters into their own hands, playing the role of God.

Nevertheless, in times of frustration, or when we don't know what to do, we must have enough faith to trust God and do nothing. Wait for God to tell you what to do if anything at all. Most times, it takes more faith to do nothing.

When we rely on our own strength and abilities, we are not using faith and are acting in the flesh. When we act in the flesh, we run the risk of pulling up the weeds and killing the wheat in the process. In other words, we may make the problems worse by trying to solve them on our own instead of allowing God to direct us.

'Trust in the LORD with all thine heart; And lean not unto thine own understanding. In all thy ways acknowledge him, And he shall direct thy paths.'
Proverbs 3:5-6 KJV

Developing an intimate relationship with God is the only way a believer can learn to truly love, believe, trust, and appreciate God. To be intimate with God we must get to know God's innermost character. This will give us the ability to distinguish God's voice from all other voices. We must keep a communication line open with God. The Father, the Son, and the Holy Spirit

'My sheep hear my voice, and I know them, and they follow me:'
John 10:27 KJV

'Examine yourselves as to whether you are in the faith. Test yourselves. Do you not know yourselves, that Jesus Christ is in you?— unless indeed you are disqualified.'
II Corinthians 13:5 NKJV

Of course, it would be a lot easier to hear God, if His voice was the only voice that we could hear. God speaks to us through our thoughts. Unfortunately, so does the Devil. Satan loves to twist the truth and turn it into a lie. Trying to figure out which voice to listen to can be challenging. We have to keep every thought under subjection, in other words, keep our thoughts in check.

Ask yourself:
- Will it please Christ?
- Does it line up with God's word?
- Are my motives pure?
- Will it help or hurt others?
- Is it convicting but not condemning?
- Do I have a sense of peace about it?
- Am I willing to have my thoughts validated by other believers?

If you answer No; to any of these questions, you will need to question the source of that thought.

There are times that I have hesitated to share what I believe that God had shown me or told me to say. People use God's name so loosely at times. However, I am learning that I cannot control what other people do or say; If they use the Lord's name in vain, they will have to answer to God for themselves.

We must realize that when God speaks through us, our voice is no longer our own, but is the voice of God and He will make the necessary corrections.

'Therefore I write these things being absent, lest being present I should use sharpness, according to the authority which the Lord has given me for edification and not for destruction.'
II Corinthians 13:10 NKJV

Don't shoot the messenger!

As a Believer and a messenger of God, I have been appointed the great burden of warning the world as well as the Church of our wrathful ways and teachings. I DO NOT by any means take this commission lightly, because I know that I am held to an even greater standard.

'My brethren, let not many of you become teachers, knowing that we shall receive a stricter judgment. ' James 3:1 NKJV

The deep convictions that God has placed in my heart compels me to help us free ourselves of the guilt and shame, to help stop the harsh punishment and the physical and verbal abuse that God's little disciples have to endure, which have been and are still, turning our children's hearts away from God instead of toward Him.

Jesus desires that we walk in the newness of life. He wants us to possess and portray the fruit of the Spirit and to demonstrate them throughout our lives and teach our children to do the same. As faith-filled parents, we should be part of the solution and not a part of the problem.

Don't take my word for it. Test the Spirit by the Spirit, ask the Holy Spirit to reveal its authenticity.

'Beloved, do not believe every spirit, but test the spirits, whether they are of God; because many false prophets have gone out into the world.' I John 4:1 NKJV

'Be anxious for nothing, but in everything by prayer and supplication, with thanksgiving, let your requests be made known to God; ' Philippians 4:6 NKJV

Testimonial

I thank the almighty God for His love, His grace, and His mercy. I thank God for His redemption power through faith in the precious blood and resurrection of Christ Jesus. I thank Him for sending His Holy Spirit as a guide and counselor.

Even though I have made Christ my Lord and Savior, from a very early age. I have not always had my current perspective on the "ROC" The Rod Of Correction. Although in my heart I have always felt something just wasn't right.

"Spare The Rod Spoil The Child" had been beaten into me so, that I almost felt like I was doing my children a disservice by not whipping them. Even perhaps sinning by not beating them or causing them to go to hell.

'Apply thine heart unto instruction, And thine ears to the words of knowledge. Withhold not correction from the child: For if thou beatest him with the rod, he shall not die. Thou shalt beat him with the rod, And shalt deliver his soul from hell. My son, if thine heart be wise, My heart shall rejoice, even mine. '
Proverbs 23:12-15 KJV

But thank God for Jesus! He showed me a better way. The Lord showed me a clear picture of the characteristics and intent of Scriptures concerning the "ROC", Jesus, The Living Word of God, and the love, peace and freedom that comes along with it.

You see, it is the devil's typical (MO) motive of operation to twist the Word of God for his own agenda. Just like he did from the very beginning with Adam and Eve. He mixes a little bit of truth with a whole lot of lies. Yes, we must use the "ROC" to correct, instruct, and teach our children. Beat them day and night with the Word of God, the weapon of the Spirit, instead of beating them with the weapons of man.

Only the Holy Spirit can change a person's heart. Satan is so conniving. He even tried to tempt and convince Jesus to commit suicide while He was fasting in the wilderness. Satan tried to use the Scriptures, God's own Word out of context. Therefore, you know Satan doesn't mind trying to deceive us.

'and saith unto him, If thou be the Son of God, cast thyself down: for it is written, He shall give his angels charge concerning thee: And in their hands they shall bear thee up, Lest at any time thou dash thy foot against a stone.'
Matthew 4:6 KJV, Psalms 91:11-12 KJV

There were a lot of mixed emotions that I experienced with the raising of my children. My former husband and I barely spanked our children. As a matter of fact, when our children were younger, we didn't have to spank them because they were such well-mannered children. When we took them out to restaurants and other public places, we would always get compliments on how well-behaved they were.

The children's father was in the military. He weighed about 220 pounds, and he could bench press around 350 pounds, so he didn't do much whipping. He was all bark and no bite. Unfortunately, he could be a bit condescending and overbearing at times. Even though we both come from a Christian background, we had our own share of harsh discipline; therefore, I believe we tried to spare our children that experience. It's not that we didn't believe in physical punishment. The truth is, I don't even remember discussing the issue.

The girls were in ballet school and life seemed to be going pretty well that was until, God turned my world up-side down when he placed this deep conviction against harsh physical and verbal discipline in my heart. I didn't know at that time if the thoughts were really coming from God or if I was being deceived by the Devil. So, I asked the Holy Spirit to confirm it, and I dived into God's Word. I would pray about it daily. Before long God began to lift the veil through dreams, visions, and through His Word. I began to share with the children's father about what God was showing me. He would not entertain the idea for one second. I will not forget the look that he gave me.

That created a foothold for the Devil. That was ok. I began to apply even more positive parenting strategies. The children and I started attending church more frequently. When it came to disciplining my oldest daughter, all I had to do with her was raise my voice and she would cry like she lost her best friend, and she would fall in line. She wasn't used to my authoritative voice. With my second baby girl, discipline was not as easy. She was a very strong-willed child. She just wouldn't listen. She always had to learn things the hard way. My oldest daughter learned what not to do by watching my baby girl. However, I didn't have to spank her much, but I always had a prayer in my heart concerning her. I had to trust God on how to discipline her because she would get on my last nerve. By the way, this is something that you should NEVER tell a child though I am guilty of it.

When my second born would be disobedient, something unpleasant would always happen to her. Most of the time it was instantly, and I knew it was God and so did she. I would remind her that God does not like ugly and how God felt about her being disobedient to her parents. Then she would fall in line as well. Even to this day she has a high respect for God because of those experiences.

God was still talking to me. I was still writing things down. I was still fact checking and consulting with the Holy Spirit, and He was still confirming His Word. Soon God would reveal to me that it was for a book. I was excited but concerned. I have never considered myself a storyteller or a writer. However, with God's help it was all coming together; that is until *LIFE* happened, and all hell began to break loose.

The Devil's foothold was quickly giving the Devil a leg-up. Marital problems began, the arguing and the aggression, unfortunately, a lot of times in the presence of the children. We were going through midlife crisis, and spiritual struggles. I had a miscarriage, had some health issues, my parents passed away, financial issues, and terrible teens, my house burned down with about most of the material for this book inside, including the floppy disc. Just problem after problems.

In between all of that our son was born. He was an unexpected answer to prayer. I had always wanted a son, but I figured I wouldn't try for one, seeing that my mother had five girls, and my marriage wasn't adding up to be all that I thought it would be.

Even though I didn't agree with my parents' discipline tactics, in my moments of weakness and frustration I still spanked my children a time or two because I didn't know what else to do. That didn't happen too often because after whipping my children I was more tired and more beat than they were. Half of the time I would overhear them telling each other that it didn't even hurt. Yet my heart would be racing. I would be out of breath. I felt like I needed a nap.

Dealing with the weight of the guilt was more exhausting than anything else. It didn't help that the children were getting big enough to whip me, and if I hadn't instilled the fear of God in them at an early age, I could see how this could have posed a problem.

My son was the sweetest little boy. However, I feel like I didn't do enough to protect him or prepare him from the verbal abuse in our home or the bullying in our environment we had to become accustomed to after separating from their father at that time.

I have always tried to use positive discipline with my children because of my own childhood trauma. However, there have been a few moments of weaknesses that I regret to this day, especially concerning my son. He seems to have the most bottled-up anger and like me, he loves to fight. He even boxes as a hobby. I think it's an outlet, and that he would be the next Suga-Ray Leonard if given the chance.

When it comes to discipline, sometimes you may need to get a little creative. As the children grew older, we would use discipline methods like taking away privileges such as: phones, games, and other electronics, and limiting TV time. We would do time-outs or maybe increase chores. We would restrict visits from friends, going outside and going to other social events. We have even removed the bedroom doors when necessary. In my opinion, all these disciplinary strategies were just as effective as whipping without all the drama and the risk of causing physical harm or assisting spiritual pollutants to enter their spirits.

I remember a time when I was still living at home with my parents. I was twenty years old and too big to whip anymore. My father must have been led by the Holy Spirit. My dad got pretty clever with his disciplinary tactics.

I had my own job and I had purchased my own car, but I was covered under my parent's insurance. I would call myself sneaking out of the house at night and had the nerves to be behind on my insurance payments. Incidentally this particular night (to my surprise) when I went to sneak out of the house with my keys in my hand, I looked out the door, and all I saw was my poor little car with all four of the tires off and was sitting on concrete blocks.

I couldn't even get mad. I was so out done. All I could do was go to bed. My dad taught me a lesson that night that I will never forget. Now every time I think about this story, I just can't help but laugh.

Discipline is a hard thing to figure out. That is why we must be willing to let the Holy Spirit lead and guide us with this very crucial matter.

If there were things that I could do over with my children, I would have consulted with the Holy Spirit for EVERYTHING. I really believe that I would have used more positive parenting methods. I would have taught my children more about Jesus. I would have taken them to Sunday School more often, and I would have spent more quality time with my children in their teenage years.

I was working really hard to just maintain. Although I was operating my own business, going through a divorce, and dealing with the distractions of life, I neglected to depend on God to lead and guide me for a time. I was trying to do everything within my own strength, which was not a good idea.

But thank God for Jesus because He was there all the time. I was just too busy focusing on my past and my issues to see that.

Regardless of all that, embracing my rich inheritance of holiness that my parents left me and teaching my children the standard of holiness and about the love of God was the best thing I have ever done.

All three of my children are God fearing adults. They have respect for their elders and people in general. They don't have a police record, nor are they hooked on drugs to my knowledge. They don't cause me any stress or give me anxiety like some children due to their parents, even after they are all grown-up.

My son is a good man. He is independent with good work ethics and will make a great husband and father one day.

My girls are hard-working women, wonderful wives, and awesome mothers, who try to implement more positive parenting strategies in their home also. They are trying to break this cycle of barbaric behavior. I know it is only by the grace of God. They may not be perfect, just as I am not perfect. However, I thank God for keeping his promises.

'Train up a child in the way he should go: And when he is old, he will not depart from it.'
Proverbs 22:6 KJV

It has taken me almost twenty years to write this book. I have been in spiritual warfare using the weapons of man. I have been distracted with life's ups and downs. I thought that all hope was lost for writing this book after my house burned down with what I thought was all the notes and materials for it. To my surprise earlier this year my sister came across the only content left for my book at our family home. *It was the partial manuscript that I had given to my mother to read.*

God revealed to my spirit that it was now time to complete the work that He had begun in me.

'being confident of this very thing, that he which hath begun a good work in you will perform it until the day of Jesus Christ:'
Philippians 1:6 KJV

The road to freedom did not come overnight for me. Even though I could see the way, walking it was a different story. I have spent most of my adult life trying to heal from the wounds of life, which included forgiveness, and letting go of all that bottled up anger and bitterness, forgetting about all that wrathful teaching and ways.

'Pursue peace with all people, and holiness, without which no one will see the Lord: looking carefully lest anyone fall short of the grace of God; lest any root of bitterness springing up cause trouble, and by this many become defiled; ' Hebrews 12:14-15 NKJV

The Lord showed me that sometimes good people can do bad things. If we are not careful, we all can have moments of weakness. We can be deceived by the enemy. We can go through life viewing things with a distorted perception, looking from behind a veil like Moses did and not even know it.

I am thankful for my Savior and Lord Christ Jesus and the counsel of the Holy Spirit within me. I am truly grateful that God has lifted the veil from my eyes, allowing me to become consciously aware of the many dangers in the misuse of Scriptures, and the dangers physical and verbal punishment poses on our children and on their guardians. I am so thankful that even though I may feel unworthy, God has deemed me worthy. God has placed His trust in me to share His message of love and peace, His grace and mercy to the world and to the Church.

'So shall My word be that goes forth from My mouth; It shall not return to Me void, But it shall accomplish what I please, And it shall prosper in the thing for which I sent it.'
Isaiah 55:11 NKJV

I pray that this book will be a blessing to the readers and that the Holy Spirit will confirm, convict, and convince. I believe that God's Word will accomplish all that it is purposed to achieve. I pray that the Lord will continue to use me as He sees fit. In Jesus Name. Amen.

Survey Results

My purpose for performing a survey on the topic of child discipline is because I wanted to know if there were others who feel like I do, those who believe that there must be a better way to discipline our children, who have had doubts about whether or not God is pleased with the physical punishment of our children, or if God is even the reason why parents whipping and beating our children as a disciplinary method as supposedly stated in the Bible.

After collecting and reviewing the data from the surveys and interviews I have determined that I am not alone. People/parents worldwide, and from all walks of life, have strong opinions and beliefs about child discipline but yet, they are not really certain if physical punishment is beneficial or harmful.

Less than 20% of surveying respondents believe that God literally wants us to physically beat our children as a form of discipline, regardless of age, sex, race, religion, and other influential factors.

The majority of surveying respondents, especially among those aged 40 and older with religious affiliations, believe physical punishment is an acceptable form of discipline, they even believe that it can be beneficial, but they also agree that it can also be damaging.

More than 95% of surveying respondents agree that alternative disciplinary methods work regardless of age, sex, race, religion, and other influential factors. Therefore, trying to understand why people risk the potential damage of physical punishment, especially if alternative methods of discipline are just as effective, has been my challenge.

I have concluded that many parents just know that something must be done in order to get their children's attention to make them behave or even keep them safe. I believe that many parents have unconsciously developed the herd-mentality and have adopted the normalcy of physical punishment.

Furthermore, I feel that there is a misperception on the effectiveness of physical punishment, and a lack of awareness on the potential damage of physical discipline. Many different experiences in life have shaped many parents' perspective on child discipline, as well as the deficiency of education on the subject of applying obtainable alternative disciplinary methods that have proven successful.

Fortunately, after many individuals began to answer the survey questionnaire below, it seems that they were encouraged to reflect on their own childhood experiences and disciplinary practices that they implement; this led them to question, why they believed as they believe.

Many people seem to become consciously aware of the potential harmful effects of physical punishment. Several individuals have expressed to me that after looking back, they probably would have considered doing things much differently and plan to explore different methods of discipline in the future.

Survey

Hi, my name is Claudie Holmes, I am an aspiring author. I am conducting a 5–10-minute anonymous survey that I would love for you to complete.

There are a few closed-ended questions, some open-ended questions, along with a few short answers. The information that I gather will be used solely for my upcoming book.

The survey is on the sensitive, controversial, and age-old topic of child discipline. How child discipline strategies vary depending on one's religion, race, social status, age, culture, and sex? How does it affect one's physical, mental, emotional, spiritual, and psychological health? How has it evolved over time? Are there alternative options available for disciplining that work?

Questionnaire

1. Age: _____
2. Sex: _____
3. Religion:

   _____

4. Race/ Races:

   _____

5. Economic status: Above average? _____
   Average? _____ Below average? _____

6. Place of origin:

   _____

7. Were you raised in a single parent home? _____

8. Were you spanked as a child? ___

9. If yes, how?

   _____

10. Do you feel whipping was beneficial or damaging?

    _____

11. Do you approve of physical discipline?

    _____

12. Why? or why not?

    _____

13. Have you tried alternative disciplinary methods? _____

14. If so, what?

    _____

15. Do you believe that alternative discipline is effective? _____

16. Do you Believe God literally wants us to physically "beat" our children? _____

17. Why or why not?

    _____

18. What do you believe is the determining factor between whipping and abuse?

    _____

19. Comments:

    _____

Glossary

Abuse- The improper use of something, cruel and violent treatment of a person or animal. Insulting and offensive language.

Adoration- Deep love and respect.

Admonition- An act or action of admonishing; authoritative counsel or warning, reproof, rebuke, chastisement, reproach.

Affirmations- The action or process of affirming something or being affirmed, emotional support or encouragement.

Anger- A strong feeling of annoyance, displeasure, or hostility.

Beat- Strike (a person or an animal) repeatedly and violently so as to hurt or injure them, typically implemented with something such as a club or whip. To defeat, to succeed in, rhythm, movement, to pulsate, completely exhausted.

Believe- Accept (something) as true, hold (something) as an opinion.

Believers- a person who believes that a specified thing is effective, proper, or desirable.

Confess- admit or state that one has committed a crime or is at fault in some way.

Consequences- A result or effect of an action or condition.

Correction- The action or process of correcting something.

Church folks- Religious people, or groups.

Devilment- reckless mischief; wild spirits.: "his eyes were blazing with devilment".

Discipline- Training (someone) to obey rules or a code of behavior, a branch of knowledge, typically one studied in higher education.

Double Entendre- word or phrase open to two interpretations, one of which is usually risqué or indecent.

Faith- Strong belief in God or in the doctrines of a religion, based on spiritual apprehension rather than proof.

Fear- an unpleasant emotion caused by the belief that someone or something is dangerous, likely to cause pain, or a threat.

God The Father- the creator and ruler of the universe and source of all moral authority; the supreme being.

God The Holy Spirit- (in Christianity) the third person of the Trinity; God as spiritually active in the world.

God The Son- Jesus Christ, Our Lord, the Messiah, the Savior, the Son of God, The Lamb of God, the Good Shepherd, the Redeemer, the Prince of Peace.

Herd-Mentality- The tendency for people's behavior or beliefs to conform to those of the group to which they belong.

Holiness- The state of being holy.: "a life of holiness and total devotion to God".

Instruction- A direction or order, detailed information telling how something should be done, teaching, education.

Knowledge-awareness or familiarity gained by experience of a fact or situation, facts, information, and skills acquired by a person.

Metaphor- a figure of speech in which a word or phrase is applied to an object or action to which it is not literally applicable.

Parables- a simple story used to illustrate a moral or spiritual lesson, as told by Jesus in the Gospels.

Paradoxes- a seemingly absurd or self-contradictory statement or proposition that when investigated or explained may prove to be well founded or true.

Proverbial- (of a word or phrase) referred to in a proverb or idiom.

Punishment- the infliction or imposition of a penalty as retribution for an offense.

Rearing- bring up and care for (a child) until they are fully grown, especially in a particular manner or place.

Reproof- an expression of blame or disapproval, make a fresh proof of (printed matter), correct.

Reverential- Respect the nature of, due to, or characterized by reverence.: "their names are always mentioned in reverential tones".

Rod- a thin straight bar, especially of wood or metal.: "concrete walls reinforced with steel rods.

Satan- (in Christian and Jewish belief) the chief evil spirit; Satan.: "belief in the Devil" "the work of the Devil"

Savior- A person who saves someone or something (especially a country or cause) from danger, and who is regarded with the veneration of a religious figure

Scornful- Feeling or expressing contempt or derision.

Society- The world, the public, mankind, the aggregate of people living together in a more or less ordered community.

Spirit- The non-physical part of a person which is the seat of emotions and character, the soul.

Subliminal- Of a stimulus or mental process) below the threshold of sensation or consciousness; perceived by or affecting someone's mind without their being aware of it, hidden, concealed.

Surpass- exceed; be greater than, to outshine, to beat, to outweigh.

Teach- Show or explain to (someone) how to do something.

Train- Teach (a person or animal) a particular skill or type of behavior through practice and instruction over a period of time.

Warfare- Engagement in or the activities involved in war or conflict.

Wisdom- the quality of having experience, knowledge, and good judgment; the quality of being wise.

Whip, Spank- A thrashing or beating with a whip or similar implemental heavy blow, or the sound of such a blow. A slap.

Wrath- extreme anger.

Violence- Behavior involving physical force intended to hurt, damage, or kill someone or something.

Favorite Scriptures

Genesis

'So God created man in His own image; in the image of God He created him; male and female He created them.'
Genesis 1:27 NKJV

'And the Lord God formed man of the dust of the ground, and breathed into his nostrils the breath of life; and man became a living being.'
Genesis 2:7 NKJV

And the serpent said unto the woman, Ye shall not surely die: for God doth know that in the day ye eat thereof, then your eyes shall be opened, and ye shall be as gods, knowing good and evil.
Genesis 3:4-5 KJV

Deuteronomy

'Only take heed to thyself, and keep thy soul diligently, lest thou forget the things which thine eyes have seen, and lest they depart from thy heart all the days of thy life: but teach them thy sons, and thy sons' sons; specially the day that thou stoodest before the LORD thy God in Horeb, when the LORD said unto me, Gather me the people together, and I will make them hear my words, that they may learn to fear me all the days that they shall live upon the earth, and that they may teach their children. '

Deuteronomy 4:9-10 NKJV

'Ye shall walk in all the ways which the LORD
your God hath commanded you, that ye may
live, and that it may be well with you, and that
ye may prolong your days in the land which ye
shall possess.'
Deuteronomy 5:33 NKJV

'Hear, O Israel: The LORD our God is one
LORD : and thou shalt love the LORD thy God
with all thine heart, and with all thy soul, and
with all thy might. And these words, which I
command thee this day, shall be in thine heart:
and thou shalt teach them diligently unto thy
children, and shalt talk of them when thou
sittest in thine house, and when thou walkest
by the way, and when thou liest down, and
when thou risest up. And thou shalt bind them
for a sign upon thine hand, and they shall be
as frontlets between thine eyes. And thou shalt
write them upon the posts of thy house, and on
thy gates. '
Deuteronomy 6:4-9 KJV

'Therefore shall ye lay up these my words in
your heart and in your soul, and bind them for
a sign upon your hand, that they may be as
frontlets between your eyes. And ye shall teach
them your children, speaking of them when
thou sittest in thine house, and when thou
walkest by the way, when thou liest down, and
when thou risest up. And thou shalt write them

upon the door posts of thine house, and upon thy gates: '
Deuteronomy 11:18-20 KJV

A woman shall not wear anything that pertains to a man, nor shall a man put on a woman's garment, for all who do so are an abomination to the Lord your God.
Deuteronomy 22:5 NKJV

'Gather the people together, men, and women, and children, and thy stranger that is within thy gates, that they may hear, and that they may learn, and fear the LORD your God, and observe to do all the words of this law: and that their children, which have not known any thing, may hear, and learn to fear the LORD your God, as long as ye live in the land whither ye go over Jordan to possess it.'
Deuteronomy 31:12-13 KJV

I Chronicles
'Saying, "Do not touch My anointed ones, And do My prophets no harm."'
I Chronicles 16:22 NKJV

II Chronicles
If My people who are called by My name will humble themselves, and pray and seek My face, and turn from their wicked ways, then I will hear from heaven, and will forgive their sin and heal their land.
II Chronicles 7:14 NKJV

Psalms

Blessed is the man Who walks not in the counsel of the ungodly, Nor stands in the path of sinners, Nor sits in the seat of the scornful;
Psalms 1:1 NKJV

'The Lord tests the righteous, But the wicked and the one who loves violence His soul hates.'
Psalms 11:5 NKJV

'Cease from anger, and forsake wrath; Do not fret— it only causes harm.'
Psalms 37:8 NKJV

'Indeed, they belch with their mouth; Swords are in their lips; For they say, "Who hears?"'
Psalms 59:7 NKJV

For he shall give his angels charge over thee, To keep thee in all thy ways. They shall bear thee up in their hands, Lest thou dash thy foot against a stone.
Psalm 91:11-12 KJV

'Your word is a lamp to my feet And a light to my path.'
Psalms 119:105 NKJV

'Behold, children are a heritage from the Lord , The fruit of the womb is a reward.'
Psalms 127:3 NKJV

'Like arrows in the hand of a warrior, So are the children of one's youth.'
Psalms 127:4 NKJV

Proverbs
'Trust in the Lord with all your heart, And lean not on your own understanding; In all your ways acknowledge Him, And He shall direct your paths.'
Proverbs 3:5-6 NKJV

'My son, give attention to my words; Incline your ear to my sayings. Do not let them depart from your eyes; Keep them in the midst of your heart; For they are life to those who find them, And health to all their flesh.'
Proverbs 4:20-22 NKJV

'He who spares his rod hates his son, But he who loves him disciplines him promptly.'
Proverbs 13:24 NKJV

'A soft answer turns away wrath, But a harsh word stirs up anger.'
Proverbs 15:1 NKJV

'The tongue of the wise uses knowledge rightly, But the mouth of fools pours forth foolishness.'
Proverbs 15:2 NKJV

'The eyes of the Lord are in every place, Keeping watch on the evil and the good.'
Proverbs 15:3 NKJV

'A wrathful man stirs up strife, But he who is slow to anger allays contention.'
Proverbs 15:18 NKJV

'The heart of the wise teaches his mouth, And adds learning to his lips. Pleasant words are like a honeycomb, Sweetness to the soul and health to the bones.'
Proverbs 16:23-24 NKJV

'A fool's mouth is his destruction, And his lips are the snare of his soul.'
Proverbs 18:7 NKJV

'Death and life are in the power of the tongue, And those who love it will eat its fruit.'
Proverbs 18:21 NKJV

'Chasten your son while there is hope, And do not set your heart on his destruction. A man of great wrath will suffer punishment; For if you rescue him, you will have to do it again.'
Proverbs 19:18-19 NKJV

'Blows that hurt cleanse away evil, As do stripes the inner depths of the heart.'
Proverbs 20:30 NKJV

'Thorns and snares are in the way of the perverse; He who guards his soul will be far from them.'
Proverbs 22:5 NKJV

'Train up a child in the way he should go: And when he is old, he will not depart from it.'
Proverbs 22:6 KJV

'He that soweth iniquity shall reap vanity: And the rod of his anger shall fail. '
Proverbs 22:8 KJV

'Foolishness is bound in the heart of a child; But the rod of correction shall drive it far from him. '
Proverbs 22:15 KJV

'Apply thine heart unto instruction, And thine ears to the words of knowledge. Withhold not correction from the child: For if thou beatest him with the rod, he shall not die. Thou shalt beat him with the rod, And shalt deliver his soul from hell. My son, if thine heart be wise, My heart shall rejoice, even mine. '
Proverbs 23:12-15 KJV

'The rod and reproof give wisdom: But a child left to himself bringeth his mother to shame. '
Proverbs 29:15 KJV

Ecclesiastes
'Do not let your mouth cause your flesh to sin, nor say before the messenger of God that it was an error. Why should God be angry at your excuse and destroy the work of your hands? '
Ecclesiastes 5:6 NKJV

Isaiah
'So shall My word be that goes forth from My mouth; It shall not return to Me void, But it shall

accomplish what I please, And it shall prosper in the thing for which I sent it.'
Isaiah 55:11 NKJV

Matthew

'and saith unto him, If thou be the Son of God, cast thyself down: for it is written, He shall give his angels charge concerning thee: And in their hands they shall bear thee up, Lest at any time thou dash thy foot against a stone.'
Matthew 4:6 KJV

'From that time Jesus began to preach and to say, "Repent, for the kingdom of heaven is at hand."'
Matthew 4:17 NKJV

'In this manner, therefore, pray: Our Father in heaven, Hallowed be Your name. Your kingdom come. Your will be done On earth as it is in heaven. Give us this day our daily bread. And forgive us our debts, As we forgive our debtors. And do not lead us into temptation, But deliver us from the evil one. For Yours is the kingdom and the power and the glory forever. Amen.'
Matthew 6:9-13 NKJV

'Therefore, whatever you want men to do to you, do also to them, for this is the Law and the Prophets.'
Matthew 7:12 NKJV

'Let them alone. They are blind leaders of the blind. And if the blind leads the blind, both will fall into a ditch."'
Matthew 15:14 NKJV

'At that time the disciples came to Jesus, saying, "Who then is greatest in the kingdom of heaven?" Then Jesus called a little child to Him, set him in the midst of them, and said, "Assuredly, I say to you, unless you are converted and become as little children, you will by no means enter the kingdom of heaven. Therefore whoever humbles himself as this little child is the greatest in the kingdom of heaven. '
Matthew 18:1-4 NKJV

'Whoever receives one little child like this in My name receives Me. "Whoever causes one of these little ones who believe in Me to sin, it would be better for him if a millstone were hung around his neck, and he were drowned in the depth of the sea. Woe to the world because of offenses! For offenses must come, but woe to that man by whom the offense comes!'
Matthew 18:5-7 NKJV

Mark
'Assuredly, I say to you, whoever does not receive the kingdom of God as a little child will by no means enter it." '
Mark 10:15 NKJV

'Jesus answered him, "The first of all the commandments is: 'Hear, O Israel, the Lord our God, the Lord is one. And you shall love the Lord your God with all your heart, with all your soul, with all your mind, and with all your strength.' This is the first commandment. And the second, like it, is this: 'You shall love your neighbor as yourself.' There is no other commandment greater than these."'
Mark 12:29-31 NKJV

Luke
'And He spoke a parable to them: "Can the blind lead the blind? Will they not both fall into the ditch? '
Luke 6:39 NKJV

'A disciple is not above his teacher, but everyone who is perfectly trained will be like his teacher. And why do you look at the speck in your brother's eye, but do not perceive the plank in your own eye? Or how can you say to your brother, 'Brother, let me remove the speck that is in your eye,' when you yourself do not see the plank that is in your own eye? Hypocrite! First remove the plank from your own eye, and then you will see clearly to remove the speck that is in your brother's eye.'
Luke 6:40-42 NKJV

'Verily I say unto you, Whosoever shall not receive the kingdom of God as a little child shall in no wise enter therein. '
Luke 18:17 NKJV

John

'In the beginning was the Word, and the Word was with God, and the Word was God. He was in the beginning with God. All things were made through Him, and without Him nothing was made that was made. '
John 1:1-3 NKJV

'And the Word became flesh and dwelt among us, and we beheld His glory, the glory as of the only begotten of the Father, full of grace and truth.'
John 1:14 NKJV

'For God so loved the world, that he gave his only begotten Son, that whosoever believeth in him should not perish, but have everlasting life.'
John 3:16 KJV

'For God sent not his Son into the world to condemn the world; but that the world through him might be saved. He that believeth on him is not condemned: but he that believeth not is condemned already, because he hath not believed in the name of the only begotten Son of God. '
John 3:17-18 KJV

'My sheep hear My voice, and I know them, and they follow Me. '
John 10:27 NKJV

Romans

'For the wages of sin is death, but the gift of God is eternal life in Christ Jesus our Lord.'
Romans 6:23 NKJV

'For I know that in me (that is, in my flesh) nothing good dwells; for to will is present with me, but how to perform what is good I do not find. '
Romans 7:18 NKJV

'For Christ is the end of the law for righteousness to everyone who believes.'
Romans 10:4 NKJV

'That if thou shalt confess with thy mouth the Lord Jesus, and shalt believe in thine heart that God hath raised him from the dead, thou shalt be saved. For with the heart man believeth unto righteousness; and with the mouth confession is made unto salvation. '
Romans 10:9-10 KJV

'So then faith comes by hearing, and hearing by the word of God.'
Romans 10:17 NKJV

'I beseech you therefore, brethren, by the mercies of God, that ye present your bodies a living sacrifice, holy, acceptable unto God, which is your reasonable service. '
Romans 12:1 KJV

'And be not conformed to this world: but be ye transformed by the renewing of your mind, that ye may prove what is that good, and acceptable, and perfect, will of God. '
Romans 12:2 KJV

'Repay no one evil for evil. Have regard for good things in the sight of all men. If it is possible, as much as depends on you, live peaceably with all men. '
Romans 12:17-18 NKJV

'Beloved, do not avenge yourselves, but rather give place to wrath; for it is written, "Vengeance is Mine, I will repay," says the Lord. '
Romans 12:19 NKJV

'Do not be overcome by evil, but overcome evil with good.'
Romans 12:21 NKJV

'Owe no one anything except to love one another, for he who loves another has fulfilled the law. For the commandments, "You shall not commit adultery," "You shall not murder," "You

shall not steal," "You shall not bear false witness," "You shall not covet," and if there is any other commandment, are all summed up in this saying, namely, "You shall love your neighbor as yourself." Love does no harm to a neighbor; therefore love is the fulfillment of the law.'
Romans 13:8-10 NKJV

1 Corinthians

'But God hath revealed them unto us by his Spirit: for the Spirit searcheth all things, yea, the deep things of God. For what man knoweth the things of a man, save the spirit of man which is in him? even so the things of God knoweth no man, but the Spirit of God. Now we have received, not the spirit of the world, but the spirit which is of God; that we might know the things that are freely given to us of God. Which things also we speak, not in the words which man's wisdom teacheth, but which the Holy Ghost teacheth; comparing spiritual things with spiritual. But the natural man receiveth not the things of the Spirit of God: for they are foolishness unto him: neither can he know them , because they are spiritually discerned. But he that is spiritual judgeth all things, yet he himself is judged of no man. For who hath known the mind of the Lord, that he may instruct him? But we have the mind of Christ.'
1 Corinthians 2:10-16 KJV

2 Corinthians

Therefore, if anyone is in Christ, he is a new creation; old things have passed away; behold, all things have become new.
II Corinthians 5:17 NKJV

'Examine yourselves as to whether you are in the faith. Test yourselves. Do you not know yourselves, that Jesus Christ is in you?— unless indeed you are disqualified. '
II Corinthians 13:5 NKJV

'Therefore I write these things being absent, lest being present I should use sharpness, according to the authority which the Lord has given me for edification and not for destruction.'
II Corinthians 13:10 NKJV

Galatians

'But if you are led by the Spirit, you are not under the law. Now the works of the flesh are evident, which are: adultery, fornication, uncleanness, lewdness, idolatry, sorcery, hatred, contentions, jealousies, outbursts of wrath, selfish ambitions, dissensions, heresies, envy, murders, drunkenness, revelries, and the like; of which I tell you beforehand, just as I also told you in time past, that those who practice such things will not inherit the kingdom of God.'
Galatians 5:18-21 NKJV

'But the fruit of the Spirit is love, joy, peace, longsuffering, kindness, goodness, faithfulness, gentleness, self-control. Against such there is no law. '
Galatians 5:22-23 NKJV

'Brethren, if a man is overtaken in any trespass, you who are spiritual restore such a one in a spirit of gentleness, considering yourself lest you also be tempted. Bear one another's burdens, and so fulfill the law of Christ. '
Galatians 6:1-2 NKJV

'Do not be deceived, God is not mocked; for whatever a man sows, that he will also reap. For he who sows to his flesh will of the flesh reap corruption, but he who sows to the Spirit will of the Spirit reap everlasting life. '
Galatians 6:7-8 NKJV

<u>Ephesians</u>
'For we are His workmanship, created in Christ Jesus for good works, which God prepared beforehand that we should walk in them.'
Ephesians 2:10 NKJV

'Be angry, and do not sin": do not let the sun go down on your wrath, '
Ephesians 4:26 NKJV

'nor give place to the devil. '
Ephesians 4:27 NKJV

'Let no corrupt word proceed out of your mouth, but what is good for necessary edification, that it may impart grace to the hearers. '
Ephesians 4:29 NKJV

'And do not grieve the Holy Spirit of God, by whom you were sealed for the day of redemption. Let all bitterness, wrath, anger, clamor, and evil speaking be put away from you, with all malice. And be kind to one another, tenderhearted, forgiving one another, even as God in Christ forgave you.'
Ephesians 4:30-32 NKJV

'Children, obey your parents in the Lord: for this is right. Honor thy father and mother; which is the first commandment with promise; that it may be well with thee, and thou mayest live long on the earth. And, ye fathers, provoke not your children to wrath: but bring them up in the nurture and admonition of the Lord. '
Ephesians 6:1-4 KJV

'Finally, my brethren, be strong in the Lord, and in the power of his might. Put on the whole armour of God, that ye may be able to stand against the wiles of the devil. For we wrestle not against flesh and blood, but against principalities, against powers, against the rulers of the darkness of this world, against spiritual wickedness in high places. Wherefore

take unto you the whole armour of God, that ye may be able to withstand in the evil day, and having done all, to stand. Stand therefore, having your loins girt about with truth, and having on the breastplate of righteousness; and your feet shod with the preparation of the gospel of peace; above all, taking the shield of faith, wherewith ye shall be able to quench all the fiery darts of the wicked. And take the helmet of salvation, and the sword of the Spirit, which is the word of God: praying always with all prayer and supplication in the Spirit, and watching thereunto with all perseverance and supplication for all saints; '
Ephesians 6:10-18 KJV

Philippians
'being confident of this very thing, that He who has begun a good work in you will complete it until the day of Jesus Christ; '
Philippians 1:6 KJV

'that you may approve the things that are excellent, that you may be sincere and without offense till the day of Christ,'
Philippians 1:10 KJV

'Brethren, I count not myself to have apprehended: but this one thing I do, forgetting those things which are behind, and reaching forth unto those things which are before, I press toward the mark for the prize of the high calling of God in Christ Jesus.'

Philippians 3:13-14 KJV

'Be anxious for nothing, but in everything by prayer and supplication, with thanksgiving, let your requests be made known to God; '
Philippians 4:6 NKJV

Colossians
'Children, obey your parents in all things: for this is well pleasing unto the Lord. '
Colossians 3:20 NKJV

'Fathers, provoke not your children to anger, lest they be discouraged. '
Colossians 3:21 NKJV

I Thessalonians
'For God hath not appointed us to wrath, but to obtain salvation by our Lord Jesus Christ, '
I Thessalonians 5:9 KJV

'See that no one renders evil for evil to anyone, but always pursue what is good both for yourselves and for all.'
I Thessalonians 5:15 NKJV

I Timothy
'Let no one despise your youth, but be an example to the believers in word, in conduct, in love, in spirit, in faith, in purity. '
I Timothy 4:12 NKJV

II Timothy

'Study to shew thyself approved unto God, a workman that needeth not to be ashamed, rightly dividing the word of truth. '
2 Timothy 2:15 KJV

'But continue thou in the things which thou hast learned and hast been assured of, knowing of whom thou hast learned them; and that from a child thou hast known the holy scriptures, which are able to make thee wise unto salvation through faith which is in Christ Jesus.'
2 Timothy 3:14-15 KJV

'All scripture is given by inspiration of God, and is profitable for doctrine, for reproof, for correction, for instruction in righteousness: '
2 Timothy 3:16 KJV

Hebrews

'For the word of God is quick, and powerful, and sharper than any twoedged sword, piercing even to the dividing asunder of soul and spirit, and of the joints and marrow, and is a discerner of the thoughts and intents of the heart. '
Hebrews 4:12 KJV
'if they fall away, to renew them again to repentance, since they crucify again for themselves the Son of God, and put Him to an open shame.'
Hebrews 6:6 KJV

'Now faith is the substance of things hoped for, the evidence of things not seen. '
Hebrews 11:1 NKJV

'But without faith it is impossible to please Him, for he who comes to God must believe that He is, and that He is a rewarder of those who diligently seek Him.'
Hebrews 11:6 NKJV

'And you have forgotten the exhortation which speaks to you as to sons: "My son, do not despise the chastening of the Lord, Nor be discouraged when you are rebuked by Him; For whom the Lord loves He chastens, And scourges every son whom He receives." Now no chastening seems to be joyful for the present, but painful; nevertheless, afterward it yields the peaceable fruit of righteousness to those who have been trained by it.'
Hebrews 12:5-6,11 NKJV

'Pursue peace with all people, and holiness, without which no one will see the Lord: looking carefully lest anyone fall short of the grace of God; lest any root of bitterness springing up cause trouble, and by this many become defiled; '
Hebrews 12:14-15 NKJV

James

'If any of you lacks wisdom, let him ask of God, who gives to all liberally and without reproach, and it will be given to him. But let him ask in faith, with no doubting, for he who doubts is like a wave of the sea driven and tossed by the wind. '
James 1:5-6 NKJV

'So then, my beloved brethren, let every man be swift to hear, slow to speak, slow to wrath; for the wrath of man does not produce the righteousness of God.'
James 1:19-20 NKJV

'But be ye doers of the word, and not hearers only, deceiving your own selves. For if any be a hearer of the word, and not a doer, he is like unto a man beholding his natural face in a glass: for he beholdeth himself, and goeth his way, and straightway forgetting what manner of man he was. '
James 1:22-24 KJV

'My brethren, let not many of you become teachers, knowing that we shall receive a stricter judgment. '
James 3:1 NKJV

'But no man can tame the tongue. It is an unruly evil, full of deadly poison. '
James 3:8 NKJV

'With it we bless our God and Father, and with it we curse men, who have been made in the similitude of God. Out of the same mouth proceed blessing and cursing. My brethren, these things ought not to be so.'
James 3:9-10 NKJV

I John
'Beloved, do not believe every spirit, but test the spirits, whether they are of God; because many false prophets have gone out into the world. '
I John 4:1 NKJV

'There is no fear in love; but perfect love casteth out fear: because fear hath torment. He that feareth is not made perfect in love. '
1 John 4:18 KJV

References and Resources

National Child Abuse Hot Line
(800) 422-4453

National Data Archive on Child Abuse
and Neglect
http://www.ndacan.cornell.edu/

Understanding Child Emotional Abuse
https://kidshelpline.com.au/parents/issu
es/underst...

Child Abuse and Neglect. Centers for
Disease Control and Prevention
https://www.cdc.gov/violenceprevention/
childabusea...

988 Suicide & Crisis Lifeline
https://988lifeline.org/?utm_source=goo
gle&utm_medium=web&utm_campaign
=onebox

Step by Step Guide to Understanding
the Cycle of Violence
https://domesticviolence.org/cycle-of-
violence/

Florida Department of Education,
Phone: 850-245-0505
https://www.fdle.state.fl.us/MSDHS/Mee
tings/June-Meeting-
Documents/Presenta

Florida Department of Education
tions/June-7-1045AM-DOE-Olivia-
School-Discipline.aspx

Studie.com, Corporal Punishment:
History & Effects
https://study.com/academy/lesson/corpo
ral-punishment-history-effects.html#

Psychology Today, Psychological
Slavery
https://www.psychologytoday.com/us/bl
og/family-secrets/201405/psychological-
slavery

The Willie Lynch Letter and The Making
of a Slave
https://www.saberesafricanos.net/phoca
downloadpap/libros/Lets_Make_A_Slav
e_The_Making_Of_A_Slave.pdf

PSYCHOLOGY BENEFITS SOCIETY
https://psychologybenefits.org/2017/02/0
1/why-do-parents-physically-punish-
their-
children/#:~:text=From%20a%20parenta
l%20cognitive%20perspective,is%20an
%20effective%20teaching%20tool.

Positive Parenting Solutions
https://www.positiveparentingsolutions.c
om/discipline/the-spanking-debate-
continues

Very Well Family
https://www.verywellfamily.com/what-is-
authoritative-parenting-5270916

(800) KRAV MAGA 1-800-572-8624
https://www.kravmaga.com/the-best-
self-defense-classes-for-safe-and-
strong-kids/

Master Hope Ozimek 850-816-1144
White Tiger Taekwondo & Fitness
Protection Connection
https://wttkdpace.com/

Youversion Bible app
https://my.bible.com/moments

Your Dictionary
https://www.yourdictionary.com/

Mightier
https://be.mightier.com/articles/affirmations-for-kids/

Gabby A Big Aill
https://gabbyabigaill.com/50-biblical-affirmations-that-will-change-your-life/#:~:text=Introducing%20Biblical%20Affirmations&text=God%20is%20not%20human%20to,power%20to%20change%20your%20life.

Mental Notes

_____

_____

_____

_____

_____

_____

_____

_____

_____

_____

_____

_____

_____

_____

_____

_____

_____

_____

_____

_____

_____

Mental Notes

Acknowledgments

I would like to thank all of you who have taken the time to purchase and read this book. I truly believe that it will be a blessing to you and your family. Please share it with as many people as you can, so they too can be blessed.

I truly appreciate everyone that has completed a survey, an interview or just shared their opinions. I would like to thank my family, church family, friends, students, and coworkers whose impactful words have encouraged me to complete this.

I would like to give a special thanks to my precious cousin Bobby Richburg and my sister V Renae Holmes for helping me put my thoughts and beliefs into comprehensible verbiage that others can understand.

I would also like to give a special thanks to my sister from another mother; Myra Richburg, to my former husband and his wife; Carlos and Cotina Modley, and to my wonderful fiancé; TK Bostick a beautiful man in the Lord, for their unwavering love and support, for their prayers, and for lending an ear and a shoulder when I needed it the most. But most of all, I thank God for the inspiration of the Holy Spirit and the opportunity to be used by Him and to serve Him and His people.

Made in the USA
Columbia, SC
24 June 2023

19045912R00109